THE BAFFLED PARENT'S GUIDE TO

Sibling Rivalry

Contemporary Books

Chicago New York San Francisco Lisbon London Madrid Mexico City

Milan New Delhi San Juan Seoul Singapore Sydney Toronto

The McGraw·Hill Companies

Library of Congress Cataloging-in-Publication Data

Borden, Marian Edelman.
    The baffled parent's guide to sibling rivalry / Marian Edelman Borden.
        p.   cm.
    Includes bibliographical references.
    ISBN 0-07-141226-3
    1. Child rearing.   2. Sibling rivalry.   3. Interpersonal conflict in children.
4. Social skills in children.   5. Brothers and sisters.   I. Title: The baffled
parent's guide to sibling rivalry.   II. Title.

HQ769.B653   2003
649'.143—dc21   2003043819

*For John
with love and gratitude for everything, and most especially
for sharing the wonder, excitement, and fun
of raising Charles, Sam, Dan, and Maggie*

1 2 3 4 5 6 7 8 9 0   AGM/AGM   2 1 0 9 8 7 6 5 4 3

ISBN 0-07-141226-3

Interior design by Think Design Group

McGraw-Hill books are available at special quantity discounts to use as premiums and
sales promotions, or for use in corporate training programs. For more information, please
write to the Director of Special Sales, Professional Publishing, McGraw-Hill, Two Penn
Plaza, New York, NY 10121-2298. Or contact your local bookstore.

This book is printed on acid-free paper.

Contents

Preface

"I don't understand how people learn to live in the world if they haven't had siblings. Everything I learned about negotiation, territoriality, co-existence, dislike, inbred differences, and love despite knowledge I learned from my four younger siblings."

—Anna Quindlen, author, *Siblings*

When you have your first child, you're overwhelmed. You can't figure out how one little person can have such an enormous impact on your life. Then you have your second child, and you can't figure out what was so hard about having just one. As one mother remarked after the birth of her second baby, she could either brush her teeth or wash her hair in the morning, but not both.

Having a second child doesn't just double the work; somehow it's an exponential increase. Couple that with constant exhaustion and the feeling that you are being pulled in a million directions, and it's hard to underestimate the magnitude of having more than one child. Yet most of us wouldn't miss the experience for the world. We want our children to know the warmth, strength, comfort, and encouragement of having a sibling.

Let's be honest. Research has shown that only children grow up just fine. They're not any more likely to be maladjusted or lonely than anyone else. But research has also clearly demonstrated that the greatest gift you can give your firstborn is a sibling. This book confirms that and then helps you navigate the often-tricky shoals of raising more than one child.

There are many, many people to thank for their help and cooperation in writing this book. First, thanks to my older sister, Rachel, for all her love and support and her clear demonstration of what a sibling relationship can be. Also, many thanks to my four children, Charles, Sam, Dan, and Maggie, who show me daily the complex but delightful world of siblings. This book would not have been possible without the insight and generosity of many parents and experts who shared their own experiences and practical advice in raising more than one. While many asked to remain anonymous, special thanks to Thea Beaver, Tina Brogadir, Wendy Brooks, Betsy Cherkasky, Tricia Duffy, Colleen Davis Gardephe, Leslie Garfield, Elaine Kellogg, Micki Kushner, Kate Kelly Schweitzer, Toby Sklarew, Kathy Staudt, and Marlo Wiggans.

Thanks, too, to Judith McCarthy, an extraordinary editor, who suggested this project.

As always, no book would be possible without the help and support of my husband and friend, John Borden.

The journey of raising more than one child is long, complicated, exhausting, and incredibly rewarding. Enjoy!

PART ONE

Since Cain and Abel

CHAPTER 1

All Parents Are Baffled Some of the Time

When I gave birth to my second child, Sam, I wrote five pages in my personal journal. Rereading that entry, I discovered that I never once mentioned the new baby. Instead, I wrote in great detail about all my fears and concerns about what I had done to Charles, my firstborn. What, I asked, were we thinking when my husband and I decided to give that sweet little boy a sibling? Had we ruined his life? Chalk up the melodrama to postpartum hormones, but I seriously worried that Charles would be confused and jealous—and he was. I feared he would feel abandoned and angry—and he probably did a little. And I expected he would never forgive his parents for bringing this interloper into our happy household—but he did!

But the one emotion I never wrote about was how Charles was also, at least eventually, relieved and grateful for this new addition to the family. Relieved that the full-time, all-consuming, at times smothering parental attention was finally, at least partially, diverted to someone else. And grateful, because he now had an ally, a buddy, a comrade in arms to traverse this life with him.

Of course, by the time I had my third son, Dan, and then a few years later, my daughter, Maggie, I'd learned a lot about siblings and the way they interact and affect each other's lives. I also discovered I didn't have much time to write in personal journals!

At Wit's End

"It is with our brothers and sisters that we learn to love, share, negotiate, start and end fights, hurt others, and save face."

—Jane Mersky Leder, author,
Brothers and Sisters

I found that I could follow all the suggestions about how to avoid sibling jealousy, and the result would be the same. One child would tell me that I wasn't fair and that another sibling (name supplied by the angry child) always got (fill in with the ensuing litany demonstrating that the scales of justice had been seriously unbalanced). I could stand in the kitchen and count out the number of peas on each plate and still, I'd be accused by one disgruntled offspring that he was being forced to eat more than his allotted share while I was permitting a sibling to coast through life without touching a green vegetable.

There have certainly been countless occasions when the older siblings have reminded me that I have "no standards left, Mom," when I've permitted a younger sibling to watch a television show that the older ones claim would have been off-limits in their "youth." Upon finding a carton of chocolate milk in the refrigerator, two older boys gasped in horror that I was pumping sugar directly into the veins of their younger siblings. Of course, after complaining, they immediately reached for glasses for themselves, albeit with grumblings about how "you never bought this for us when we were little."

Yes, don't you just love siblings?

This book is intended to help you navigate the minefield that having more than one child inevitably creates. But if you think it's going to answer all your questions, let me be honest. It can't. Because, as you've learned since the arrival of your first child, raising kids is often a fly-by-the-seat-of-your-pants experience. You've got to trust your instinct, because the most important lesson you'll ever learn about parenting is that you know your kids best. The ideas and suggestions you find in this and any other parenting book are just that—suggestions. They've worked before, maybe even often. They're certainly worth consideration. But if your gut tells you that the advice doesn't apply to your child, I'd bet you're right.

It's true that sometimes we're too close to a situation to be able to judge it effectively. To be certain, make a list of the pros and cons of the course of action, step back, and then you can decide. But don't assume that the experts know more than you. When it comes to your kids, you are the expert!

The Advantages of Having a Sibling

Research has shown that having a sibling provides definite emotional and developmental benefits:

- On a simple level, a sibling provides ready, available companionship. As many hours as parents are willing to devote to entertaining their child, kids enjoy the company of their peers.
- Fantasy play, so important in a child's development, is more fun with another youngster at about the same developmental stage.
- More importantly, having a sibling means being part of another child's world. An only child tends to live in an adult world because the child interacts so much with grown-ups.
- Living with a sibling teaches critical negotiating skills. Brothers and sisters learn about compromise—and they learn how to make up.

The Bottom Line

With siblings, rivalry is inevitable. It doesn't matter how good a parent you are, your kids will at some point want your attention exclusively, and that is the underlying basis of most sibling conflict. Children often see parental love as a zero-sum game. There's only so much to go around, and any love bestowed upon one sibling means less for another.

Of course, parents know that their hearts expand. Realistically, the birth of a new child will mean less time for the older one, but it does not mean less love. Convincing a youngster of that fact is the most important element of reducing sibling rivalry.

It's About Time

The number of years between your children will almost inevitably affect their relationship. How much they argue and how well they play together will be influenced by how close they are in age. But age is only one of the factors.

Did You Know?

Having siblings may increase your chance of becoming president of the United States. Forty out of forty-three U.S. presidents had siblings. The remaining three—Franklin Delano Roosevelt, Gerald Ford, and Bill Clinton—were the only offspring of their parents but had half-siblings. President James Buchanan had the most siblings: four brothers and six sisters.

At Wit's End

"Your sister is the only creature on earth who shares your heritage, history, environment, DNA, bone structure, and contempt for stupid Aunt Gertie."

—Linda Sunshine, author

If your children are close in age, born less than fifteen months apart, you may face many of the same issues as a family with twins. If the children are more than five years apart, you may be dealing with two "only" children, who enjoy the advantage of also having siblings.

There really isn't any ideal spacing. Health issues for the mother and baby might arise if the pregnancies are too close together. Women who have given birth by cesarean section and then get pregnant again with an interval of eighteen months or less between the two deliveries have a threefold increased risk of uterine rupture compared with women whose deliveries are further apart. Babies conceived within six months after a previous birth show a higher incidence of low birthweight and prematurity than infants conceived eighteen to twenty-three months following the last baby. Some research suggests that spacing children four years apart reduces sibling rivalry, but there are n[...] and cons to having your children spaced [...] apart. You need to decide what works best f[...]

Close Together

Parental ages, careers, temperaments, finance[...] and circumstances may influence the decisi[...] together (less than eighteen months between [...] times feel like you're in the middle of "all babi[...] at some point, that stage is over! Here are s[...] closely spaced kids:

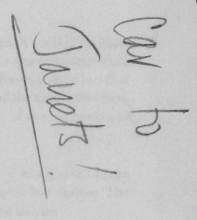

- The house is baby-proofed, diaper-ready. Y[...] and bottles, and you may even have adjuste[...] baby stage is compressed and intense—but [...]
- Your oldest child doesn't get used to being a [...] child. The adjustment to a new baby may be easier.
- The children have built-in playmates.

Of course, there are also disadvantages to being close in age:

- Children close in age may be treated as a unit, rather than as individuals, and there may be less recognition of the differences in age and development.

- Parents may be so exhausted from the demands of two children so close in age that they may have difficulty enjoying some of the early stages.
- There are fewer opportunities for one-on-one time with each child.

More Years in Between

Now consider the advantages of spacing further apart (two years or more):

- Older children can better understand the needs and demands of a baby.
- The older sibling may be verbal enough to articulate his feelings, able to entertain himself for periods of time, helpful to the parent, and depending on age, able to dress himself and toilet-trained.
- Having a much younger sibling allows an older child (or children) to participate in younger kinds of play. The older children can still enjoy toys they might otherwise think of as babyish.
- The older child can be a nurturer and teacher.
- Parents are likely to feel less stressed and more financially secure.
- Siblings who are at least two years apart fight less.

The disadvantages of spacing further apart include the following:

- The older child may have a harder adjustment changing from being an "only" to being a sibling.
- The logistics of balancing the needs of an older child with the demands of a baby are more complex. For example, parents may feel that the baby never gets a nap because they are always waking her so they can take the older one somewhere.
- Different developmental levels may make it difficult for siblings to enjoy playing with each other for extended periods of time. But they can enjoy some things together like building with blocks, playing with the computer, cooking. These differences even out as children grow older and share more experiences.
- Siblings with a large age difference don't interact as much as those who are closer in age.

Did You Know?

George Foreman has five sons, all named George (Junior, III, IV, V, VI), as well as five daughters (Michi, Freeda George, Georgetta, Natalie, and Leola).

Cleopatra had five siblings. Her older sister was also named Cleopatra, as was her mother. Her two younger brothers, both named Ptolemy, were named after their dad—whose name was . . . Ptolemy.

Personality Influences

Whether your children are less than a year apart or more than five years apart, the personalities of all the parties—kids and parents—will play a significant role in how well the siblings get along. It's not a matter of good or bad. Some parents just have more easygoing temperaments, and having kids close together in age doesn't bother them. Similarly, some children are more high maintenance than others, so it wouldn't matter if there were ten months or even five years between siblings. Parenting would still be tough.

In this section, *high-maintenance* or *high-needs* refers to children with personalities that are charitably called determined, exciting, intense, and active. At less-pleasant moments, they might be described as negative, exhaustively challenging, not very adaptable, and hypersensitive. In this sense, *high-needs* is a question of temperament, personality, and style, not a chronic illness or disability. See Chapter 10 for more on the latter situation.

Ideally, for smooth sibling interactions, a high-maintenance child would be matched with a low-maintenance sister or brother. (Or even better, you'd have two low-maintenance kids and two low-needs parents!) But what frequently happens is that a couple has one baby who's fairly easy to manage, then when the parents decide to expand the family, they get the baby from hell. How often have you heard second-timers comment, "If this had been my firstborn, it would have been my only"? It's almost as if the fates, determined that humans should reproduce, give a pass on the firstborn's temperament and dial up the intensity for baby number two, on the assumption that experienced parents should be better able to handle it. Of course, sometimes the high-maintenance child is the firstborn—and then you just count your lucky stars when you get an easier baby the next time around. You've earned it.

But how does the high-low combination affect the sibling interaction? Parents usually worry, sometimes with good reason, that the high-needs child will dominate the family, preempting her less-demanding sibling, sort of like Lucy and Linus in "Peanuts." That could happen, and you need to be conscious of the situation so that you give enough attention to each child. But just because one child is louder or more exhausting, it doesn't necessarily mean that the quieter, less obviously demanding offspring is being shortchanged. She may be perfectly happy not being the center of attention. That could be her style.

If one child repeatedly garners more attention because of bad behavior toward her sibling, you have to consider the reasons for the misbehavior. Then tailor your response accordingly:

Great Idea!

Get organized to reduce sibling rivalry. If you set up your older child in some play activity *before* you have to take care of the younger sibling—for example, giving her markers and paper so she can draw while you are feeding the baby—she's less likely to try to demand attention.

- Is the child misbehaving out of a belief that it's the only way she can compete for your attention because her sibling is (according to her) smarter, prettier, more athletic, funnier, firstborn, the baby, all of the above? In other words, is your child acting out in order to force the spotlight away from her sibling because she feels that she doesn't shine otherwise? (Remember, her concerns don't have to be true; what is important is that she genuinely believes them.) If so, it's up to you to make sure that each child feels special and valuable on her own. Boosting a child's diminished self-esteem can reduce tensions.
- Parents may not be the cause of the jealousy. Kids draw their own conclusions, even with the best of parental efforts to minimize sibling comparisons. Don't underestimate the influence of friends, teachers, extended family, the media, even strangers. All help form a child's self-image. For example, if one child is more petite than her sibling and others often comment on it, those comments can make a huge impact on both children, even if you never mention size at all. Make sure that you understand how your child views himself. You'll need to counterbalance any negative input he receives.

Carving Out Time for Each Child

You can reduce sibling rivalry and build a stronger relationship between your kids by separating them! When you find time to spend alone with each child, you're reinforcing each child's sense of self-worth, bolstering his self-image, and encouraging him to see that he is not just part of a group ("the kids") but an individual. This will reduce the tensions that are inevitable when kids are forced to do everything together. The child can spend the one-on-one time with either parent.

Great Idea!

Having trouble finding special time with each child? Include your children in your chores or activities. For example, if you enjoy working out, give them pretend weights so they can join you as you get your exercise and spend quality time with your youngster.

Finding the opportunity to spend "quality time" with each child in the midst of a busy schedule is often tough. Here are some tips:

- *Seize the moment*—Schedule some special time with an older sibling when the younger one is napping. It doesn't have to be every day. Parents often use the time when the baby is napping to insist that the older child play quietly, too, so that everybody gets a little time off. But if, a few times a week, you can seize the opportunity for some quality, individual time for the older one, it will pay off in reduced sibling rivalry.
- *Reduce interference*—Plan one-on-one time away from home in order to avoid one sibling interfering or intruding on another's special time.
- *Set rules*—Make clear to the siblings that each has to respect the other's time alone with the parent. Point out, with specific time and place, when each child's turn will come.
- *Stagger bedtimes*—Even just a fifteen-minute difference provides an opportunity to quietly discuss the day and concerns with each child.
- *Combine chores and one-on-one time*—Use everyday activities, such as grocery shopping, to spend time alone with each child. It's probably more efficient to shop alone, but this is an easy way to integrate one-on-one time and run an errand.
- *Include other family members*—Children need to spend quality time alone with their parents, but grandparents, aunts, and uncles can also provide moments when each child has a turn in the spotlight.

The Sibling Scene

Sibling relationships are complicated. Only on television, in those old sitcoms, do we see brothers and sisters as the best of friends. Of course, on these same shows, the dogs are well behaved, too, and they clearly have not met any of the four-legged ones in my family.

Pure harmony among siblings is not the reality for most of us. Sure, there are days when our offspring behave as if they are filming an old episode of "Leave It to Beaver," and we wonder if the pod people have invaded. But if we're smart, we're grateful for the respite from the constant bickering, squabbling, picking, and at times, physical violence. Unfortunately, those sitcom days seem to be few and far between.

Siblings relate to each other in a wide variety of ways. Many influences, coming from within and outside of the family, affect this precious relationship.

It's All Relative

Do genetic traits make it more likely that your children will share similar interests and therefore relate better? If the kids look alike, are they more likely to be better friends? And if they're not biologically related, what are the chances that they'll be close?

Genetics plays a minor role in the creation of a strong sibling relationship. Much more important is that the kids share an environment and a common family history. Who else besides a sibling will remember

At Wit's End

"If sisters were free to express how they really feel, parents would hear this: 'Give me all the attention and all the toys, and send Rebecca to live with Grandma.'"

—Linda Sunshine, author

11

Great Idea!

Accentuate the positive. Praise a child when he is behaving well around his siblings, so he associates good behavior with parental attention.

the name of your third-grade teacher, the color of the living room drapes, and that disastrous car trip to the beach?

Growing up together has a much greater impact on the sibling relationship than genes. Furthermore, your children don't need to share the same interests in order to be close. In fact, having separate areas of excellence might reduce competition.

Size Counts

The sibling relationship is also affected by the size of the family. While those closest in age may share a tighter bond, this isn't always true. Common interests and gender also play an important role in how close individual siblings become. One advantage of coming from a family of four or more children is that, frankly, the siblings have a larger group from which to choose. Children from large families often speak of "always having someone to play with," but this is tempered by the admission that "there's never any privacy." Both statements are usually reflected in sibling relationships.

Parental stress levels generally increase with the addition of each child, and this, too, can affect how brothers and sisters interact. The more children in a family, the greater the parental stress, which inevitably affects the family roles youngsters play. These changes include the demands on each child and the siblings' responsibilities for one another.

Siblings as (Best) Friends

"We're best friends." It would be wonderful if siblings believed that, but it's not necessarily realistic. Siblings can be close but still find comfort and support outside of the family. In fact, that is healthy. You want your children to develop separate lives and have friends beyond the immediate family.

Even so, a good sibling relationship is like a good, healthy friendship: supportive, nonjudgmental, cooperative, and loving. That's how you hope your children will be. If they turn out to be best friends as children, terrific. But it's not a mark of failure if they're not.

Frequently, siblings who as children could barely tolerate being in the same room with each other find that when they have grown up, they have a lot more in common than they had realized. Age differences no longer are as important. One woman recalls that the nearly six-year difference between herself and her older sister was almost insurmountable when they were young. Her sister was in high school while the woman was still in elementary school. Fast-forward fifteen years, and both sisters were having babies (a day apart). At that point, they became very close—best friends, in fact.

At Wit's End

"Like branches on a tree we grow in different directions yet our roots remain as one. Each of our lives will always be a special part of the other."

—Anonymous

Birth Order Impact

A great deal of research has focused on the issue of birth order and its impact on a child's personality, as well as the child's role within the family. Certain tendencies and characteristics are associated with each place in the family—oldest, youngest, and middle. Birth order can influence the way a child thinks, responds emotionally, and looks at the world, especially in terms of how the child relates to others.

However, birth order is but one of the issues that affect familial relationships. Gender, spacing, personality types, physical attributes or disabilities, birth order position of parents, blended families, and parental relationships also play vital roles in the complex sibling interactions. For example, if the oldest child in the family is a boy and the youngest is a girl, the impact of being the oldest or youngest is different compared to a family with a different combination of sexes. In a family with three children, the dynamics would be different if they were all boys or all girls, rather than if the oldest, for example, were a boy, the middle child a girl, and the youngest another boy. The middle-child syndrome would be different because the youngster would be the only girl in the family—another unique role to play. Another example of possible influences would be a younger brother being significantly bigger than his older brother, or smarter, or more athletic. And if any sibling is physically or mentally disabled, the disability will affect the dynamics of the sibling relationship and mute the impact of birth order.

Birth order characteristics may be evident in sibling twins, even though the age difference may be only a matter of minutes. However,

Of the U.S. presidents, 52 percent have been first-borns. Of the first twenty-three astronauts sent into space, twenty-one were either firstborns or only children (who have many of the same characteristics as a firstborn). Only four U.S. presidents have been the babies of their families.

other powerful influences between twins (or other multiples) may be more important than birth order. (See Chapter 10 for more information on twins and multiples.) Furthermore, a child who is the older or younger sibling of a set of twins may find her normal place in the family usurped because of the added interest in "the twins."

Of course, none of these patterns are written in stone. You've met the child who didn't seem to get the report on what role he was supposed to play in his family. Maybe it's a middle child who thinks he's a firstborn and acts just like it! But it does help to understand the basic characteristics of each birth placement because often the personality types do run true to form and do influence sibling relationships.

The Firstborn

There's a reason why so many firstborns become presidents of the United States. These first children are typically perfectionists, serious, critical, and well organized. (Of course, you may also know firstborns who are complete slobs with no focus. Remember, these are only generalizations, but they do seem often to be true.) Firstborns tend to share some other characteristics:

- Firstborns can be intense and high-maintenance.
- They can feel enormous pressure to succeed, both from their parents and from within themselves.
- The oldest often is told that he is the role model for the family.
- The firstborn sometimes serves as the substitute mother or father to the younger brothers and sisters.
- The oldest may also feel that the younger kids in the family get off easy, that less is expected of them, that he had to pave the way for the other children in the family.

Because the firstborn has your undivided attention until his sibling is born, you measure and worry about each step of his development. That focus builds his self-confidence and leadership skills but makes him understandably jealous when the attention shifts to a younger sibling. He may act out and argue with his sibling because he's angry, jealous, resentful, and insecure about his place in the family. Your job, as the par-

ent, is to reassure him and offer unconditional love, no matter how provocative the behavior.

The message always has to be clear: you love him, even if you don't like his behavior. You will not let him hurt his younger siblings, no matter how angry, even justifiably, he may be. Children are frightened when they are out of control; your job is to help them stay within the boundaries of acceptable behavior.

Firstborn Problems and Solutions The oldest child often perceives that you heap praise on the younger sibling for actions barely worth mentioning. And while parents understand that age differences justify different chores, responsibilities, and privileges, what you say is often not what your child hears. Here are some examples, followed by solutions that work:

Parent: "Look at Danny pull himself up. He's so strong."

What she hears: "Mom thinks it's neat that my baby brother can pull himself to stand, but she didn't even notice that I climbed to the top of the jungle gym. Now that's *really* strong!"

Solution: Don't fall into the trap of feeling you can't be excited by your younger child's accomplishments, even if they seem small next to what your older one is doing. Nor do you have to try to compliment the older child every time you praise one of her siblings. But occasionally it helps to gently remind the firstborn that when she was little, you noticed those same developments. Pull out her baby pictures, and show her what she was doing and how she looked at the same age as her younger sibs.

Parent: "Make your bed."

What he hears: "You make your bed while I go and make the bed for your younger brother because I obviously like him better. You work, and he gets to watch television."

Solution: This situation requires three important steps. First, acknowledge your older child's feelings. It's reasonable for a youngster to resent his younger sibling's apparent free ride, even though the difference in age accounts for different levels of responsibility. Second, explain to your older child that when he was his younger sib's age, you made his bed for him, too. Finally, even if it seems like more work for you, have your

Did You Know?

Oldest children are overrepresented among college faculty, while youngest children are more frequently represented among writers, especially autobiographers and family historians. Middle children are generally very successful in team sports and make excellent managers because of their strong negotiating skills.

younger child help you when you are doing chores so that all kids learn that being part of a family means helping out.

The Youngest

Being the baby of the family has a lot of benefits. Less is expected of youngest children. Because parents have had practice with the firstborn, they are usually more easygoing, resulting in more-relaxed younger children. Babies of the family tend to be under less parental scrutiny than the firstborn. Of course, these children would complain that they often have more than one set of parents. Their siblings serve as extra parent figures. The youngest in the family is often known for being charming, affectionate, more carefree—in short, a "people person." On the other hand, youngest children are also frequently rebellious, spoiled, disorganized, and impatient. The following characteristics are typical of the baby's role in the family:

- The youngest may be jealous of the privileges and attention that the older sibling receives.
- The last-born may feel he can't compete with his older sibling's accomplishments.
- The baby of the family may be manipulative and know exactly which button to push to get a reaction from his older sibling—then, when confronted by parents, hide behind the facade of the poor, innocent younger sibling.
- The youngest may feel that her family doesn't take her seriously.
- The last-born is often the family—and class—clown.
- Older siblings often serve as the source of information for their younger siblings. It's from the older brother or sister that the younger children may learn about the birds and bees—although not necessarily accurately.
- The youngest is often the butt of an older sibling's put-downs. This is especially true when the firstborn is more verbal than the younger sib.

Youngest-Child Problems and Solutions The baby of the family often feels unable to measure up to more-accomplished older siblings, even if being older is clearly the reason for the different levels of competency. For instance, the preschooler sees that the older sib can read but he can't. This issue is at the root of the following problems and solutions.

Problem: The younger sibling insists on always being included in the older sibling's play dates.

Solution: It's important that the older child be able to play with friends without the younger sib. And the baby of the family needs to learn to respect his older sib's privacy. Even a young child can be taught to knock before entering a room.

Problem: The younger one's efforts never seem to measure up to her older sibling's accomplishments.

Solution: Offer praise for what she can do, and do not compare her achievements to the older one's activities. While it's reasonable to point out that she, too, will eventually be able to read chapter books when she is older, it's counterproductive to be constantly focusing on future achievements. Instead, talk about what your child *can* do, making a fuss over new successes—learning to ride a bike, swim across the pool, even just jump into the pool if she has been afraid. In other words, put the focus back on each child, not the sibling.

Problem: The youngest in the family often feels left out because his older sibs are dominating the conversation.

Solution: It's understandable, and probably not even deliberate, that older siblings control dinner table conversations. They are more verbal and can talk and think faster. But it's important that parents insist that each child have an opportunity to contribute to the conversation—and that siblings respect each other's opinions. Sometimes that means parents will have to steer the discussion to a topic to which each child can contribute. Even if there is grumbling from the older peanut gallery, it's good practice for them to learn to listen—really listen—to each other.

The Middle Child

The child who often produces the most parental guilt is the middle child. The child in the middle is easy to overlook when confronted with the dazzling firstborn and the endearing baby of the family. But that's OK, because the middle child is often the most competent of the group and frequently the peacemaker. The role the middle child gets to play

Trouble Zone!

Don't assume that the middle child wants to be the negotiator or that the oldest will be the leader or the baby of the family will be the charmer, based on the characteristics associated with each place in the family. Research on birth order is interesting and may be helpful in understanding behavior, but it is a generalization and may not apply to your child.

may vary. It's one of the advantages—and disadvantages—of being the middle child. This child may be linked to the oldest or tied to the youngest. Here are some other characteristics:

- The middle child may exhibit the characteristics of the firstborn, the youngest, or both. He may be serious and intense like the oldest, outgoing and carefree like the youngest, or a combination. He's the swing player in the group—he can go either way.
- While often playing the peacemaker in the family, middle children may go out of their way to avoid conflict. If she is the peacemaker, she learns strong negotiating tactics.
- In an effort to make a place for himself, the middle child is sometimes the rebel in the family.
- Being the middle child can be the best of both worlds. There's someone to look up to, while at the same time someone looks up to you.

Middle-Child Problems and Solutions Being the middle child, especially if all the kids are the same gender, can sometimes mean getting lost in the crowd. You're not the oldest; you're not the baby. The middle child's fear is, of course, "What makes me special?" The job of parents is to answer that question, making sure that each child feels he has a unique place in the family. See how that mission applies in the following situations:

Problem: The middle child resents being lumped with the youngest, even if it's appropriate.

Solution: Don't fall into a child-imposed guilt trap. As the parent, use your judgment to determine whether bedtimes, chores, and outings are appropriate for each child and, just as important, for the family as a whole. One mother of three closely spaced kids (at one point, she had three kids under three years old) needed to have all kids in bed at the same time at night for her own sanity. That's fine, too.

Problem: The middle child is constantly being drawn into the battles between the oldest and youngest.

Solution: While middle kids are often strong negotiators, make sure that's not the role they always play in the family. No one should be saddled with the sole responsibility of making peace among the siblings. Insist that warring siblings resolve their own disputes without always drawing on the talents of the middle child.

Playing Favorites

Parental favoritism can create long-term problems in sibling relationships. Of course, no parent deliberately sets out to favor one child over another. But sometimes it is easier to get along with one of your kids for a variety of reasons. He may be more easygoing in general; he may be more like you or someone you love. Conversely, you may have trouble connecting with one of your children. Perhaps that child sometimes reminds you of a relative with whom you have had a troubled relationship and pushes every button that sets you off. Sometimes, the problem is that the parent and child don't seem to have much in common. The parent is a great athlete, while the child prefers to read. Also, the child you favor can change over time—and frequently does.

In a study by researchers at Cornell University and Louisiana State University, more than 80 percent of older mothers admitted having a favorite among their grown children, and about 80 percent of the kids said they always knew it. But here's the kicker: when asked which child was the mother's favorite, most adult children got it wrong! Children were correct in identifying their mother's favorite only 41 percent of the time.

The problem is less that you have a favorite but more what you do about those feelings. And that's what's tricky. You need to make sure that each child believes she has a special place in your heart. Undoubtedly there will be times when one of your kids is easier to deal with and you feel guilty because it's more relaxing to spend time together than with your other children. But here are the important points to remember:

- Don't compare your children or offer one child's behavior as a model for the other.
- Give hugs and kisses to all your children—perhaps a few more to one who is out of favor.
- Always apply the same rules to all the children. Children should understand the consequences of misbehavior. No one gets a pass, not even one who is currently the pet.
- Discover what is special about each of your children. Sometimes a common interest with one of your kids is obvious, but find something to share with each one so that they get your undivided attention, too.

Trouble Zone!

Just as you are careful not to play favorites with your children, make sure that your baby-sitter doesn't either. Listen and ask for specific examples if one child complains that the sitter prefers her sibling. Follow up, if necessary, with your caregiver.

Play detective. Introspection can be tough, but determine why you are having difficulty relating to one of your children. If it's her behavior that is bothering you, check: is she misbehaving because she is trying to get your attention? Is your favoritism creating a sense of insecurity, which is prompting poor behavior?

Grandparents' Favorites

Sometimes grandparents play favorites. It gets even more complicated in a blended family (see Chapter 11). But parents need to be alert to the hurt feelings and sibling rivalry that can be exacerbated by grandparents who clearly prefer or indulge one grandchild over another.

They may not play favorites intentionally. The grandmother who raised two sons may be thrilled with having a granddaughter. The grandson who loves football might find a special place in a grandfather's heart.

Tactfully, but deliberately, parents must insist that grandparents treat the children equally in terms of gifts and time spent together. Furthermore, if you believe the grandparents are treating one of your kids unfairly, try to discuss the situation with them. Your job is to protect your child. If the behavior persists, as your children get older, talk openly about their feelings and perceptions. If you can't change the adult behavior, it's important that you acknowledge the emotions of the children who are affected.

PART TWO

The Art and Artistry
of Sharing

CHAPTER 3

Sharing Rooms

One mother observed that, when her sons went off to college, they had an easier time adjusting to dorm life than many of the students she met. She thinks it helped that they were part of a large family of five boys. They had always shared rooms and had learned to cope and study in the midst of chaos—the very definition of dormitory life.

However, sharing space—whether it's between siblings or even a husband and wife—is an adjustment. Frankly, just spending that much time together can spark arguments. In this case, familiarity often does breed contempt. At the very least, it makes the sibling roommate a ready target when a child is bored or even angry at something or someone else entirely.

Even so, as we will see later in this chapter, sharing rooms has some advantages. By sharing space, your children learn negotiating skills. This common ground forces kids to learn to compromise.

Often, siblings share rooms because of a lack of space. In recent years, a separate room for each child has become a sign of prosperity. But grandparents and great-grandparents can regale kids with stories about sharing not only a room but often a bed with their siblings. In some cultures, shared rooms are the norm. Many families consciously choose to have their kids share rooms, even when they have the extra space, because they believe it builds a strong sibling relationship, as well as fosters other important traits. Some parents believe in the family bed and choose to have their child or even children sleep with them.

Did You Know?

The average new house in the United States has 2,330 square feet of space, up from 1,500 square feet thirty years ago. The average home has three bedrooms. Of American families with kids, eight in ten have one or two children under the age of eighteen.

*"From the normal
irritations of living
together, they [siblings]
learn how to assert
themselves, defend
themselves, compromise."*

—Adele Faber and Elaine
Mazlish, authors, *Siblings
Without Rivalry*

Whether or not you choose to have separate bedrooms for each of your kids, you might want them to share some common space. Consider locating the family computer or television in a central location, such as the family room, den, basement, or simply an alcove in the living room. This is an area in which all hold equal ownership. Only the parents can declare the area off-limits to anyone. This teaches your children negotiating skills. Common ground forces kids to learn to compromise. Some families use one of their home's bedrooms to create shared space for the family. Rather than each child having a separate bedroom, the kids bunk up so the family can have a den or computer room.

More than a Place to Sleep

Bedrooms can serve many purposes. They are havens for the child who needs some privacy and temporary isolation booths for the youngster who's in the middle of a time-out. They may serve as a child's playroom, where all toys are stored. They are also often places where kids can express themselves in decorating their space. Of course, for some kids, the bedroom is their own personal island. For others, it is simply a place to sleep.

If you shared a room as a child with your sibling(s), share that experience with your kids. Acknowledge your feelings of occasional resentment, but also tell them funny stories from those years of togetherness.

The Advantages of Sharing Rooms

Necessity may force some families to have the kids bunk up with each other. One mother recalls having three kids—two boys and a girl—under the age of five, in a two-bedroom apartment. She had bunk beds and a crib in a ten- by thirteen-foot room. When the third child was born, he slept in the master bedroom in his carriage. Later, he slept in the living room for several months. Eventually, he moved in with his older brother and sister in the "kids' bedroom."

Other families choose to have the kids share bedrooms because of the benefits of sharing. One mother of two girls born seventeen months apart deliberately kept the youngsters together, even after they moved out of their tiny apartment into a four-bedroom house. She explains, "I'd always shared a room with my sister and thought it made us closer. I wanted that for my daughters."

There are several benefits of having kids share a bedroom:

- Youngsters learn early that they must cooperate and learn to negotiate space and privacy.
- Kids discover how to give and take. Finding out how to compromise is good preparation for college, jobs, and marriage.
- Children are less likely to be scared or feel isolated if they're in the same room. Sharing may reduce nighttime sleep problems.
- Siblings learn about sharing and also about respect for another's possessions—and privacy.
- Siblings build a treasure trove of memories when they share a room together.

Great Idea!

When siblings share a room, you can handle sleepovers by moving the host and guest to another room. Or ask the sibling who's not hosting to move for the night.

Can Brothers and Sisters Share Rooms?

When space is limited, parents may have to put their son and daughter in the same room. Experts believe that as long as the kids are preschoolers or younger, there are no long-term problems with mixing genders.

However, a child's sense of modesty usually begins to develop and evidence itself between the ages of four and eight. Then the issue of boys and girls sharing rooms becomes more problematic. If they must share, you will have to provide for some privacy. The section on decorating, later in this chapter, includes some tips on how to turn a single bedroom into two private zones.

Moving Baby In

Putting the new baby in the same room with an older sibling works just fine, provided you prepare the child as well as the space. You can reduce an older sibling's sense of displacement (and jealousy) by making him part of the process. If you are going to move the youngster from a crib into a "big boy" or "big girl" bed, it's helpful to make the change a couple of months before the baby is born. Take the crib down (or move it out of the room) while he adjusts to his new bed. That gives the older child time to become comfortable with the change and separates the two events—his move from the crib and the birth of a new baby. You don't want the older sibling to feel he had to give up his sleeping space for the new baby, even if that is true. Then, once the older sibling has adjusted to his new bed, let him help arrange the room (under close adult supervision), prepare the crib, and decorate the baby's area of the room.

If your children are on different nap schedules, one parent advises having them sleep in different rooms during the day. This arrangement avoids waking one up while reading or going through nap rituals with the other. At night, if both sleep through, they can share the bedroom.

You also need to stress safety when an older child shares quarters with a new sibling. Here are some tips:

- Small parts alert! Your older child may have toys that are safe for her but a real danger to her younger sibling. You need to be careful under any circumstances, but consider keeping toys and games with small parts out of the bedroom. They are a choking danger to infants, who tend to put everything in their mouths. You must be able to supervise how these are played with and that they are always put safely away. One mother tossed all tiny doll shoes when she moved her newborn into her preschooler's bedroom.

  Don't let the baby near toys that are smaller than a child's fist or toys that can fit through a cardboard toilet paper roll. Also potentially dangerous are small parts such as removable eyes and noses on stuffed toys and dolls, removable squeakers on squeeze toys, and figures and pieces that nestle in larger toys. Similarly, be careful of puzzle pieces and balloons.
- Anchor bookshelves and tall dressers to the wall.
- Remind the older sibling that she can't climb into the crib or on top of the changing table.
- Keep the diaper pail secured with a lid.
- Do not hang mirrors or picture frames above the bed or crib.
- Toy chests are hazards. If you are buying a new toy chest with a hinged lid, make sure it has a lid support that will hold the lid open in any

position—and test it. Also consider alternatives: chests with no lids, with lightweight removable lids, or with sliding doors or panels to prevent the hazard of a falling lid. To prevent suffocation, look for a chest with ventilation holes that will not be blocked if the chest is placed against the wall or a chest that, when closed, leaves a space between the lid and the sides of the chest. Establish a firm rule that kids may not climb in or hide in the toy box. Open baskets may be safer than chests, especially if a toddler is sharing a room with an older sibling.

Don't allow the baby to sleep in the bed with his older sibling. Both regular mattresses and waterbed mattresses have been associated with infant suffocation. There is an increased risk of death from the baby suffocating in a face-down position, in pillows or linens, or when the older child inadvertently rolls onto the baby. For one five-year period, the Consumer Product Safety Commission reported 250 deaths to infants twelve months and younger who suffocated while on beds, the majority on regular adult mattresses.

The danger is twofold. The infant may roll or move to the edge of the mattress so that his head or body becomes wedged between the mattress and the bed frame or wall and he cannot breathe. Or the infant, sleeping facedown, can have his nose and mouth trapped in the depression caused by the weight of his head and body. In any case, babies should be put to sleep on their backs to reduce the risk of sudden infant death syndrome (SIDS).

Install guardrails on both sides of toddler beds, and position cribs and beds so that the children can't reach windows, heaters, air conditioners, and room decorations. Keep the baby and older child's beds away from window blind and curtain cords to prevent strangling on the loop of the cord.

Moving Siblings Around

If you have decided to move your older child out of her current room in preparation for the arrival of a new baby, do so several months before the birth. You want to separate the two events so that your older one doesn't feel as if she is being forced to give up her room for the new baby.

Trouble Zone!

According to the Consumer Product Safety Commission, at least forty-five reported deaths and three incidents of brain damage have resulted from the lids of boxes or chests used for toy storage falling on children's heads or necks. Use open baskets for toys instead, especially in bedrooms.

Great Idea!

To divide a shared bedroom, consider purchasing secondhand office partitions.

Let her help decorate her new room, as much as is appropriate for her age. Before she begins sleeping in the new room, move her toys in.

If it is appropriate, transfer your child from a crib to a bed when she moves into the new room. But if she is not ready, don't rush the change. An older sibling may need the security of her crib until she adjusts to the new room.

Set Some Rules

To reduce the potential for sibling squabbling, you need to set some rules and establish some boundaries for the two roommates. When the kids are very young and not yet verbal, issues of privacy and ownership are harder to explain. Even then, it's important that you express these ideas so that they are well established as the children get older. Here are some time-tested rules:

- Each child needs to feel that he has some separate private space. It can be as small as his bed, but he can make the rule that no one is allowed on the bed unless invited.
- For older children, some families establish a schedule that permits each child to have time alone in the room. Teach the importance of knocking before entering. Also explain that the scheduled privacy time is just that: the other sibling must stay out unless there's a strong reason for needing to be in the room.
- There has to be a neutral zone both children can enter. Almost all siblings who've shared rooms can recall a story of drawing a line down the middle of the room (imaginary or with duct tape) to mark off the "battle zones." Each side was off-limits to the other, but inevitably, the older one drew the line so that the door was on his side and the younger brother or sister couldn't get in or out of his room.
- No borrowing without asking. This is a critical rule. You can decide that some toys or objects are to be shared, but each child must respect and ask permission to use the things that are deemed to belong to his sibling.
- If the children are old enough, have them draw up their own list of rules for the room, write them out, and post them.

- Eliminate some powder keg issues—noise and lighting—by providing headphones for music listening and reading lights next to each bed.

"If you don't understand how a woman could both love her sister dearly and want to wring her neck at the same time, then you were probably an only child."

—Linda Sunshine, author

The Odd Couple Share a Bedroom

One is a neat freak, the other a total slob. That was the dilemma facing a family with twin boys and a single bedroom for the two brothers. It was quite clear, from birth, that the twins had different temperaments. As they grew older, sibling arguments frequently erupted over what one considered a messy room and the other considered a normal state of affairs.

As the mother explains, "It wasn't fair to either boy to impose one standard of neatness. So we all sat down and established some basic ground rules. The messy twin had to keep his clutter on his side of the room, and once a week, the whole room had to be cleaned up. It was a good lesson in negotiation and compromise."

Difference in Ages

Siblings can have problems sharing rooms whether they are close in age or there is a significant difference in the number of years between them. But some of the same basic rules, such as the need for cooperation and respect, remain the same.

If there is a big age gap between the roommates, they may have less difficulty if they share similar interests. For example, having an eight-year-old share a room with his fourteen-year-old brother may seem like a recipe for disaster, but if the two share a common bond over sports, it may be less of a problem. In any case, don't let the older child's preferences dominate his younger sibling.

Teens and Preteens: The Rules Change

Adolescents, by their very nature, need more privacy for friends and for self-evaluation as part of personal growth. Furthermore, teens' sleep

Great Idea!

"Squatter's rights" is how one family defined its room assignments. When an older sibling was away at school or camp, younger siblings who had to share bedrooms could move into the empty room for the duration.

habits are very different from those of their younger siblings. Schoolwork is much more intense and requires more focus and concentration. Bedrooms are a natural haven for all of this, but if the space is shared, it's time to rethink some of the rules and consider alternatives.

Look around your house, and see if there is any space that you can use without adding on. For example, consider the basement—it doesn't even have to be finished. In exchange for privacy, a teen might be quite happy to clean up an area of the cellar, throw down an area rug, add a bed, desk, and dresser, and move in. Similarly, the attic could be converted. If the ceilings are too low, put the mattress on the floor.

One family developed a rotation system among the three kids and two available bedrooms. Each child had a turn in the single while the other two shared, and then they switched.

Decorating Tips for Shared Bedrooms

If space is limited or you choose to have your children share a room, you can still create zones of privacy for each sibling. Here are some ideas from decorators:

- Look up! Build a loft, which frees floor space underneath for a built-in desk or dresser. Put a curtain across the alcove under the loft bed for more private space.
- Bunk beds also give each child private sleeping space. With reading lamps mounted on the headboard or wall, each sibling can read at night without intruding on the other.
- Build a room divider that provides not only privacy but also built-in bookshelves and storage. Anchor it securely so kids can't topple it over.
- Before installing any kind of room divider, place a temporary one (for example, chairs) in the space so that you can test your plan before permanent installation.
- You can make an inexpensive room divider by hanging a shower curtain from a rod suspended from the ceiling. Another way to create a room divider is to cover a ready-made folding screen with wallpaper.

Use two coordinating patterns on the beds to provide a distinct look for each child.

- Make sure that both children have easy access to the door and get plenty of air and light.
- Paint each child's name or initial above his bed to personalize his side of the room.
- You can use coordinating, rather than matching, curtains and bedspreads to define each child's area. By using the same two colors, but in coordinating patterns, you create visual harmony while still creating separate zones.
- Give each child his own bulletin board, and let each child choose the posters and pictures he wants for his walls.

Trouble Zone!

It's too easy for siblings to get isolated from the family and each other if their rooms are completely self-sufficient. Even if each child has his own room, consider having only one computer, centrally located.

CHAPTER 4

Toys, Clothes, and More

Most kids, at some point, believe in the "touched it" rule, also known as the "saw it" rule. The fundamental premise of this rule is, If I've *ever* seen or touched the toy, it's mine, and you can't play with it.

This simple rule explains why sharing is a learned, not innate, habit. And for siblings, all possessions—toys, clothes, books, or a shriveled-up french fry on the floor of the car—fall under the umbrella of the touched-it, saw-it rule. Until ownership can be proved otherwise, the item belongs exclusively to the beholder. And from this inflexible rule many sibling fights have sprung.

Of course, the primary reason you want your kids to learn to share is that it makes them better people. But sharing is also important for the harmony of the family, as well as financially prudent. No parent wants to buy two (or more) of every item.

Sometimes the fight over a toy is really a fight for parental attention. From the moment the younger child is born, the firstborn is taught about the concept of sharing. The process is scary and frustrating at times because the first "possessions" the child has to share are Mom and Dad. The principle is soon extended to require sharing home and belongings. But what the youngster also learns is that sharing means the other person has to share stuff, too. The child may reluctantly share his trucks, then eagerly discover that his younger sister has to share her blocks. Sharing can be hard, but it can also be rewarding.

At Wit's End

Learning to Share

As a concept, sharing is introduced very early. Babies quickly learn about sharing a conversation. You talk to them, and they babble back, then you answer, and they respond. Another example is a simple game: you hand your baby a toy, and your baby hands it back to you. "May I have the bunny?" you ask. Your child proudly hands it to you. "Do you want the bunny?" you ask, then hand it back. The back-and-forth nature of these simple exchanges teaches the fundamentals of sharing.

By the time a child is two, he understands the concept of "mine." And from this appreciation spring many arguments—at home with siblings and in the park or preschool with other children.

Here are the steps to take to help your children learn to share:

- *Model good behavior*—So much of parenting is showing, rather than telling. Sharing is a concept that is best demonstrated, not discussed. It's as simple as sharing the ice-cream cone you're eating or offering your child a bite of your cookie. Let your children see their parents share a sandwich or take turns choosing which video to watch.
- *Look for nonthreatening opportunities for your children to share*— When siblings split an order of fries, rather than eat from two separate servings, it's a small lesson in the give-and-take of sharing. And don't count out the fries for each child to avoid a squabble. Try to let them work it out themselves.
- *Pile on the praise*—Catch your kids when they are willingly and nicely sharing. Then praise lavishly.
- *Allow special treatment of special items*—Don't insist that everything has to be shared or passed along to a younger sib. Even if your child has outgrown a certain toy, she may want to keep it for comfort. Baby blankets and stuffed animals often become security items to a child. Don't insist that she pass them along to a younger sib.

The Art of Sharing Toys

One family with three children under the age of five took extreme measures in a vain attempt to cut down on the bickering over toys. The par-

ents literally wrote initials on each Lego brick in order to clearly mark the ownership of each. They believed that if each child could lay claim to his toys with no sharing involved, there would be fewer arguments. But it doesn't work that way—as they quickly discovered—and emphasizing ownership wasn't the lesson they had wanted their kids to learn.

Instead, begin with the premise that the siblings will have to share at least most of their toys. It's perfectly reasonable to designate some possessions as special, for others to play with only when the owner has expressly granted permission. It's also reasonable to limit the number of toys that can get that classification. Make it clear to the siblings that those special toys are off-limits, and keep those exclusive items in the individual child's room. If siblings share a room, keep the special items on the owner's shelf or under his bed. Those exclusive toys should not be kept among the toys available for play by siblings or other children.

What about birthday or holiday gifts? When toys are brand-new, it makes sense to allow the recipient exclusivity for a certain period of time, perhaps one or two weeks. Again, if you reserve to your child the right to designate some as special, it makes sense that most of the others will go into the group of toys shared by all.

When siblings are playing together, use these strategies to help them share toys:

- Set a kitchen timer for five minutes, then have them switch. Depending on the ages of the children, they can set the timer themselves.
- Agree that toys in common spaces, like family rooms, can be used by all kids.
- Remind them of the alternative. They may forget it when in the midst of a major battle, but kids really do have more fun playing with each other than alone. Although the squabbling is irritating, most kids, when separated, beg to be allowed to play with each other again.

Playtime Smarts

Just being siblings doesn't make playing together easy. Sure, sometimes your kids will play together quietly and happily for hours, but often it starts off great and then disintegrates into an argument over something

Great Idea!

If siblings need to share a candy bar, let one divide it, and give the other first choice of which piece. This arrangement provides an incentive to be even in the division, along with a quiet lesson in sharing.

Great Idea!

Swap puzzles—and toys—
with another family. Sib-
lings get new toys without
additional cost. Set a time
limit on the exchange.

trivial. Keep in mind that siblings, unless they are twins, are not peers. The age difference may influence the sophistication of play, frustrating the older sibling because the younger one is not old enough to play the kind of game desired. The attention span of the younger one also may limit play. The younger child's antics may try the patience of the older one. Add to the mix the possibility that siblings have temperaments and personalities that tend to clash, and it's not surprising that sibling play time doesn't always go well.

You may not always be able to manage how the siblings play together, but if you can do it, planning does help relieve some of the problems. And when play does go well, the experience encourages kids to do it again. If you know that the kids will be together all day and be each other's only companions for play, try some of these ideas for making the experience pleasant for all:

- Playing outside is often easier. Running around, climbing on a jungle gym, throwing a ball, or playing soccer expends energy, and age differences are less important.
- When the kids are indoors, suggest activities such as art projects that are less competitive and permit each child to work at his own level.
- Eliminate territorial issues by encouraging them to play with the toys held in common. If they want to use their "special" toys, it's often helpful if each child brings some to the table. That way neither child feels as if only her belongings are being used.
- If "special" toys are being included in play, the owner may not deny his sibling equal use of the toy. Otherwise, take the toy out of use.
- Find projects that the siblings can do together. For example, a joint project like building a fort with blocks encourages teamwork and reduces competition.
- If there's a meltdown, call a time-out. If necessary, separate the siblings for a period of time until tempers are under control. Sometimes you can clear the air just by switching activities. Offer some quiet time like reading a book to both kids, having a snack if hunger might be part of the problem, or heading outdoors to get rid of some energy.
- If the siblings are having difficulty playing together, ask them to come up with options. Have them suggest alternative activities.

One mother of three closely spaced kids recalls that even if the weather was bad (unless there was thunder and lightning), she used to dress the kids in protective gear and head outside. "It was worth all the trouble of putting on raincoats and boots—and then having to towel-dry everybody when we returned. Just taking a walk around the block got rid of excess energy. It made them settle down and play nicely together when we came back in."

Big-Ticket Items

Especially for expensive items, kids need to learn to share. While some families may choose to buy individual computers, televisions, or video game players for each child, most prefer to see the siblings figure out how everyone can use these items fairly. Some families set up schedules, with the understanding that using the computer for schoolwork always takes precedence over its use for play.

Don't necessarily assume that if one child dominates the use of a toy, the others must be feeling deprived. It's not unusual for younger sibs to watch their older brothers or sisters play video games. One mother, disturbed that the younger child was being shortchanged, was surprised when the youngster didn't want his turn. She realized he was enjoying watching a level of competence he couldn't achieve—and would practice on his own to get better.

As children outgrow items, you might want to hand them down to younger siblings. Before you do so, however, make sure they pass all safety inspections. Clean, repair, and, if necessary, repaint bikes, skateboards, scooters, and other sports gear to make them appealing to their new owner.

Better Safe than Sorry

If your children are close in age (or multiples), you may need to have two of most baby items like cribs and car seats. Buying these products used is a good way to save money, but don't sacrifice safety standards.

Trouble Zone!

Don't skimp on safety. Before passing along a bike to a younger child, take it to a repair shop for a tune-up. Don't pass along a bike helmet without making sure it fits properly. If it doesn't fit, buy one that does.

Did You Know?

For updated information on car seat recalls, call 1-888-DASH-2DOT (1-888-327-4236) or visit www.nhtsa .dot.gov/people/injury/child ps/recall/canister.htm.

Cribs

Don't push an older child into a bed before he's ready, even if a new baby is on the way. But before you accept an older crib, make sure it meets these safety standards, recommended by the Consumer Product Safety Commission:

- A firm, tight-fitting mattress, so a baby cannot get trapped between the mattress and the crib
- No missing, loose, broken, or improperly installed screws, brackets, or other hardware on the crib or mattress support
- No more than 2⅜ inches (about the width of a soda can) between crib slats, so a baby's body cannot fit through the slats; no missing or cracked slats
- No corner posts over 1/16 inch high, so a baby's clothing doesn't get caught
- No cutouts in the headboard or footboard, so a baby's head cannot get trapped

Car Seats

Be careful of secondhand car seats, especially any that were manufactured before 1981, when the federal government adopted strict safety standards. Avoid any that have been involved in a car crash (look for cracks or other damage, although they may not be visible). Check the model number on the manufacturer's label to see if it's a model that has been recalled.

High Chairs

Before purchasing a used high chair, make sure to check for the following safety features:

- The chair should have a wide base for stability.
- The restraining straps should be in good shape and include a waist belt with a buckle that can't be fastened unless the crotch strap also is used. Look for restraining straps that are easy to fasten, to ensure their use every time. If straps are not in good shape, contact the manufacturer to replace them.

- There should be a post between the child's legs to prevent the child from slipping down and becoming trapped under the tray.

Mesh-Sided Cribs or Playpens

The Consumer Product Safety Commission recommends these safety standards for mesh-sided cribs and playpens:

- Mesh less than ¼ inch in size, smaller than the tiny buttons on a baby's clothing
- No tears, holes, or loose threads in mesh, which could entangle a baby
- Mesh securely attached to top rail and floor plate
- Top rail cover with no tears or holes
- No missing, loose, or exposed staples

The Clothing Wars

When I was pregnant with my fourth child, people often asked me if I was hoping for a girl, since I already had three sons. I'd smile and point out that I didn't mind if I had another son. After all, I had a fortune invested in boys' clothes. Of course, I was delighted when my daughter was born, but I must confess that she wore a lot of blue in the first couple of years of her life.

Certain clothes can't be classified as hand-me-downs but, rather, are sentimental favorites. I brought my oldest son home from the hospital dressed in a long-sleeved, white terry stretch suit and an undershirt, and wrapped in two receiving blankets. The poor child was probably sweltering because it was the middle of the summer and the temperature was a cool ninety-six degrees in the shade. But every other child also came home in that outfit and blankets, regardless of the season. Incidentally, for the child born in late December when the temperature was twenty degrees, I forgot the undershirt. But he was a second child, so I didn't worry!

Hand-me-down clothes are a fact of life in most families. Dress-up clothes, especially, rarely wear out. For boys of any age, navy blue blaz-

Trouble Zone!

Don't insist that a younger child wear his older sib's hand-me-downs if they are in colors or fabrics you know he dislikes. Instead, swap them with another family for an instant wardrobe without the costs. Or take your hand-me-downs to a consignment shop and use the dollars earned to buy new clothes for the younger sib.

ers with khaki or gray slacks never go out of style, and traditional-style dresses are timeless. However, one child's trendy clothes can look dated by the time a younger sibling is ready to use them. Coats, hats, and gloves can often be easily passed down through the family. Generally, avoid handing down shoes, since fit is so important. But for the rarely worn party shoes, you can make an exception. Boots can easily be reused.

Sports equipment also can be handed down, but respect sibling differences. For example, the older child may not have much interest in playing baseball, so an inexpensive mitt is just fine. But if his younger sibling is a baseball nut, then try to get him a mitt whose quality reflects that interest.

Infants and toddlers don't care if their clothes come "prestained" by an older sibling. And parents shouldn't get worried about gender stereotypes. You might get a few questions if your three-month-old son is dressed in a pink stretch suit, but any seasoned parent understands that it just makes sense to reuse layette items. As the child gets older and more aware of comments, the style and color of clothing become bigger issues.

Don't make clothes a battleground. Unless the occasion is one where attire is important to you—for example, attending worship services—let kids choose their own outfits. What they select may not be your taste, but making the decision gives them an important sense of independence. One mother recalls a constant battle over her daughter's insistence that she be allowed to wear short-sleeved T-shirts every day, even in winter. The morning struggles finally ended when the mom came up with a compromise that pleased both: the girl could wear short sleeves if she added a sweatshirt to the ensemble, which she could remove once she got to school. There are enough issues that demand firm stands between parents and child, but clothing shouldn't be one of them.

Only Hand-Me-Downs?

Once past infancy, many children become more definite about their clothing preferences. They may have a favorite shirt that they would wear daily, if given the option. Or they may refuse to wear certain types of fabrics. One youngster would wear only sweatpants because he hated the

feel of denim. For him, jeans were out of the question, whether hand-me-down or brand-new.

Adults know that wearing the right outfit can make you feel good and relaxed as you enter a new or strange situation. For example, when going on a job interview, the last thing you want to worry about is whether your suit looks flattering. It's the same thing for kids. You want to be sure they feel comfortable about their clothes when they go to a party or start the first day of school or give a recital. Give them the latitude to pick out something, assuming it's appropriate for the occasion, so that they gain that extra ounce of security.

And every child deserves something "new." It doesn't have to be name-brand or even purchased in a store, as long as it's not direct from his older sibs. With hand-me-downs from a different family or clothes from a consignment shop, he will feel like his clothes are new simply because they haven't been worn previously by a sibling.

Following are some tips to ease the clothing wars:

- Give younger siblings the right of refusal. Allow them to pick and choose which items they will wear from the clothes being handed down from an older sibling. The siblings may have very different tastes in clothing.
- To keep down costs while giving younger siblings more of a choice of hand-me-downs, swap used clothing with another family. Let siblings choose which outfits they want to wear from the household, and fill in from the hand-me-downs of another family.
- Some clothes, such as T-shirts featuring cartoon characters, get dated quickly. A child may refuse to wear a perfectly clean outfit because the decoration is "old-fashioned." Use those T-shirts for play clothes, painting smocks, or aprons.
- Make sure that hand-me-downs fit well. Replace missing buttons, hem if necessary, and work to remove stubborn stains.
- Buy new accessories to make hand-me-downs look new: for boys, a new tie to wear with the jacket from his older sibling, for girls, new tights or a sweater to dress up an outfit from an older sister. Personalize clothes when you hand them down. One mother sewed new decorative cartoon characters onto the worn coveralls she was passing down from her older son to his younger sib.

Great Idea!

Plan ahead and save money. Buy gender-neutral colors for outerwear. The pink snowsuit may look adorable on his big sister, but the younger brother will balk at wearing it.

- Respect their allegiances. Siblings may have strong preferences for different sports teams, so asking a Mets fan to wear a Yankees T-shirt is asking for trouble.
- Kids often spend an inordinate amount of time picking out their lunch boxes and backpacks. Color and decorations reflect their current tastes. If possible, let each child pick out her own, rather than passing along serviceable ones from an older sibling whose choices may not mirror those of her younger sibling.

Hand-Me-Down Etiquette

Before accepting used clothing, toys, or equipment from a friend, follow these suggestions so that there are no misunderstandings.

- *Ask if it's a gift or a loan*—Generally people don't expect clothes to be returned, but they might want back some of the big-ticket items like snowsuits, baby furniture, or sports equipment. In any case, ask. If they do, clean the item and make any necessary repairs before returning it.
- *Weigh the risk*—If the item is to be returned, consider the wear it will probably take and whether the friendship will be damaged if something happens to it. For example, will you feel comfortable using a friend's heirloom cradle? You're sure to take good care of it, but what happens if it becomes damaged? You may not want the responsibility. Consider whether you can get replacement parts if something breaks or is lost.
- *Say thanks*—Even if the other family plans to donate the items to charity if you don't take them, say thank you. You might even take a picture of your child in the item that has been lent and send it to your friend.

CHAPTER 5

Birthdays, Holidays, and Other Special Occasions

Celebrations don't always bring out the finest in kids. In the midst of a birthday party for his year-old sibling, a preschooler may have a meltdown, unable to contain his jealousy over the attention and presents directed elsewhere. It's not that children intend to intrude on their siblings' special days. Sometimes the emotions overwhelm them. But with planning, you can reduce the tantrums and increase the good times for all.

The other important issue is how involved siblings should be in each other's lives. Certainly, at special occasions like birthdays, graduations, and religious celebrations, all family members should be present. But is it reasonable to ask a child to sit through an entire season of baseball games or attend every performance of a school play in which his sibling has a bit part? There's no right or wrong answer. It's a question that parents will need to examine as they decide what works for their family. The answer may be different depending on the age of the child. The answer may also vary from one child to another.

Whose Birthday Is It Anyway?

It's a fine line: on the one hand, you want to celebrate the day each child was born, because, in fact, each birth was a joyous occasion. On the other hand, you can't ignore the feelings of jealousy and displacement that a

sibling may feel as someone else is feted. And if you can have a third hand, sometimes the birthday boy or girl isn't so generous and acts out the role of king or queen of the day, which only exacerbates a difficult situation. Juggling all these issues can be challenging, especially when the children are younger and less able to verbalize their emotions. One mother wryly recalls her four-year-old son's plaintive cry at his younger brother's second birthday: "I'm trying to be good, but it's so hard."

Party Time

If you are planning a party to celebrate a child's birthday, include the sibling in the planning. Some parents fear that asking the brother or sister to help with a sib's party will be like rubbing salt in the wound. Quite the contrary. It's a way of giving attention to the "unbirthday" child, as well as making him feel included at a time when he's apt to feel left out. Of course, you need to make sure that the birthday child understands she's in charge of her own celebration. It's always a tough balancing act with siblings!

Here are some other ways to keep that balance:

- Remind the sibling that his day—and party—will come. Bring out photos of previous celebrations, and remind him of the fun he had.
- If the birthday child is too young to help with invitations (for example, a first birthday), the older one can decorate them or put stamps on the envelopes. If there is a significant age gap between the siblings, the older one can take a more active role. The sib can help the birthday child compile the list of friends to be invited, help to decorate the room or table, or assist in preparing the food or decorating the birthday cake.
- Permit the sibling to invite a friend to the party.
- Assign the sibling a job during the party. For example, he can assist with one of the activities or distribute the food.

Gifts for and from the Sibling

One of the lessons we try to teach our kids is the joy of giving. It's a pretty heady concept for a child. Youngsters are egocentric. It's not a character flaw but a developmental stage. So it's tough to ask a child to be happy about giving another child a toy that the giver wants. Throw in the issues of sibling rivalry, and it's even harder. Even if the gift isn't one the giver particularly wants, just being in the toy store on a mission to purchase something for the sib can be difficult. But by taking each child to pick out a gift for a sibling and even having him use some of his own money to pay for it, you help to reinforce the important concept of sharing in each other's accomplishments and special days.

Of course, the gift doesn't have to be purchased in a store. Encourage the child to make a card, draw a picture, give a coupon for a story to be read or game to be played, or even to share something from his own pile of toys. The gift can even be a candy bar. The actual gift is less important than the gesture.

What about a gift for the "unbirthday" boy or girl? Some families do give a small present, or grandparents do. But it's not really necessary and probably not a good idea. Kids adjust and accept the idea that it's not their special day. However, extra hugs and reassurance are very helpful. Even more important, *praise* the older child for being such a big help at the party and for his good behavior. Acknowledge his mixed feelings on the occasion.

Christmas and Chanukah

The holidays are often a time of stress for everyone. Parents feel the pressures, but don't underestimate the effects on kids. Meltdowns are common. Not all parents celebrate the religious or spiritual aspects, but most do want their kids to come away from the season with a better understanding of the concepts of family, sharing, and giving to others. Working together to make the holidays a joyous occasion builds family unity.

Establishing holiday traditions builds a memory bank for the siblings. Don't confuse traditions with more work! If baking cookies together is something you'd like to do with your kids, you don't have to make them from scratch. Slice-and-bake cookies from the supermarket can also be easily decorated. The kids will remember the process, the fun, and the smells. The important point is that children have a concept of "This is what we do as a family to celebrate." That's the best gift you can give.

Here are some other ideas for promoting sibling harmony during the holiday season:

Great Idea!

Rather than kids returning duplicate gifts to the store, have them donate them to charity instead.

At Wit's End

"There is no ideal Christmas; only the one Christmas you decide to make as a reflection of your values, desires, affections, traditions."

—Bill McKibben, author, *Hundred-Dollar Holiday*

- Have the kids share in the holiday preparations. For example, they can help with the holiday cards. Even if parents must address the envelopes, the children can insert photos if appropriate and lick and stamp the envelopes. Let them send cards to their friends or make their own holiday cards.

- Wrapping presents for others can be a family chore. It's probably best not to have a child wrap a gift from a parent for a sibling, primarily because it might be hard for him to keep a secret! But even the smallest child can help choose the wrapping paper, hold the tape, or put a finger down to hold the ribbon in place for a bow.

- Decorating the house and preparing the holiday food are other wonderful, fun opportunities for siblings to work together.

Presents

One mother pointed out that when her kids were small, "I made sure that each child had at least one big box under the tree, no matter what was in it!" To a certain extent, she knew that when the children were young, they were counting presents, not adding up dollar figures. Older kids can understand that a video game costs fifty dollars, so even if their younger brother got five miniature cars, it doesn't add up to the cost of the one game.

You don't want to get into the Christmas Eve panic of discovering that you are one present short for one of the children and running to the grocery store to buy "something, anything" to even it up. But in general, to be realistic, when children are young, it's usually wise to buy an equal number of gifts for each.

As your kids get older and have a better appreciation for costs, it's reasonable to set a dollar amount and spend accordingly. However, it's still probably going to be hard to sell even a teenager on the idea that two compact discs are equal to the twelve packages her younger sibling got. Like everything else, parents must walk a fine line when choosing gifts for siblings.

One way families circumvent the gift dilemma is to give family gifts. The big-ticket item for the kids might be something they share, like a computer or video game player. Besides that family gift, each child gets a few small gifts.

Did You Know?

Annual sales for video game consoles and software total more than $9.97 billion. For Christmas or Chanukah, give these big-ticket items for siblings to share.

Have the children make gifts for each other, as well as for parents and grandparents. Again, the cost of the gift is irrelevant. It's even more meaningful, especially for adults, that the children give of themselves. Kids, either separately or together, could create a coupon book that promises grandparents help in gardening, cleaning up the basement, returning books to the library, even taking down holiday decorations. If they choose to make a gift, try a photo frame—all the better if you include a cute photo of the child. Parents should help each child develop a list of family and even friends they want to give to. It takes the emphasis off the gimmes and puts it on sharing.

Great Idea!

Have sibs donate books they're no longer reading to a day-care center.

Charity

Year-round, but especially during the holidays, it's important to stress the concept of caring about others, even people you don't know. Clearly, the first way to teach this value is to model the behavior. Talk to your kids about your own charitable donations. Include your kids as you drop off clothes at charity thrift shops, work in a soup kitchen, or bag lunches to be dropped off at a shelter. Take them along when you donate leftover foods or canned goods to a food pantry. Give them the change from a purchase to drop into charity cans.

At the holidays, focus on charities where your children can make a connection. For toy drives, let your children pick out a gift, wrap it, and drop it off. Donate some money to a charity that supports children's causes or, if your children are animal lovers, to a local shelter. Let them pick out some toys that they no longer play with or books that they've outgrown, assuming the items are in good condition, and take them to a homeless shelter or hospital playroom.

Halloween

One mother made an elaborate skeleton costume for her oldest son when he was four years old. The detail was impressive. So it was no surprise

Did You Know?

Halloween-related sales
rake in more than $5
billion, second only to
Christmas. Costumes
account for $1.5 billion,
with candy and accessories
making up the rest.

that his two younger brothers were expected to be skeletons when they were four years old. The middle child was perfectly happy to wear the costume, but the youngest, when it was his turn, had his heart set on being Superman. The mother had sweat equity invested in the costume, but it was an opportunity for the baby of the family to assert himself as an individual.

Let each child pick out his own costume. It's an easy way for a child to set himself apart from his siblings. Conversely, don't argue if the siblings both want exactly the same outfit. It's possible that one is influencing the other, but it's also likely that it's the current fad, which has captured their attention.

Trick or Treat

The National Safety Council recommends adult supervision for all trick-or-treaters under the age of twelve. Some families permit their children to go out on their own, *in a group*, beginning when they are ten. But don't make them responsible for supervising younger siblings. The combination of excitement, darkness, and sugar highs may make the older one less observant and the younger one too hyped up to be listening carefully. Make sure that all kids understand the safety rules:

- Children must travel only in familiar areas and along an established route that has been mapped out and given to parents.
- Children must know to stop only at houses or apartment buildings that are well lit. They are never to enter a stranger's home.
- Parents establish a firm time to come home, and kids wear a watch so they can observe this rule.
- Children understand that they may not eat any treat until a parent has inspected it.
- Parents review with the trick-or-treaters all pedestrian and traffic rules.

Sharing the Loot

All candy should be carefully inspected before being eaten. (Parents may take their favorites at this time!) Siblings often enjoy holding a swap meet at this point, trading to get more of whatever they like best. Let the kids handle the negotiations, although it's reasonable to remind everyone to be fair. Don't assume that the older one is taking advantage of his younger sibling. Often a younger sibling is willing to make what appears to be an uneven trade because he really doesn't care that much.

Other Special Occasions

Woody Allen once said, "Eighty percent of success is showing up." And for some occasions in each child's life, attendance by siblings is virtually mandatory. If it's a graduation, first communion, or bar/bat mitzvah, put on your dress-up clothes, arrive on time, and behave. That's the bottom line. To help keep these mandatory occasions peaceful, try the following suggestions:

- Remind siblings that there will be occasions when it will be their turn in the spotlight.
- Emphasize the importance of the occasion. One mother had a serious one-on-one discussion with a younger brother before his older sibling graduated. "There's no do-over to this day," she reminded him, encouraging him to be on his best behavior.
- Be sure to offer praise for cooperation.
- Pack small toys or books as a quiet distraction, and if possible, bring a snack and drink.

At other times, the issue of sibling participation is a little murkier. Is sibling attendance required at each ball game? Every piano recital? A combination of factors should influence the decision:

- Consider the child's age and temperament and the event's environment. To expect a young child to sit quietly through a two-hour piano recital, waiting for her sister to perform for three minutes or less, is asking a lot. On the other hand, that same child might be able to last through a two-hour softball game if other kids are present and she can run around a little or take some toys. Don't put a child in a situation where she can't succeed and then be frustrated when she fails to behave.

Trouble Zone!

A hungry child is generally not on his best behavior. Pack a snack of his choice when asking a child to attend a sibling's performance or game. Your best bet is a snack that takes a while to eat, such as a box of raisins.

Trouble Zone!

Trade help with another parent at recitals or other "quiet, please" events. If younger siblings are having trouble keeping still, arrange with another family to take their kids and yours outside for a walk while their older child performs, and they can return the favor when it's your older one's turn.

- Are there reasonable alternatives to taking the sibling along? Can she have a play date at a friend's house while you attend a dance recital? Can the friend drop her off at the performance just before her sister will appear? Will you have to pay a baby-sitter if she doesn't come?
- Will you enjoy the moment more if you don't have to worry about the sibling? There are times when you would like to focus on one child, without the distraction of a sibling. One parent recalls leaving a younger sibling at home with a sitter during her older daughter's school play. The mother wanted to enjoy watching her child perform and be able to attend the cast party and chat with other parents.

You want your children to be each other's best cheerleaders, but make sure you put them in situations in which they can do just that. If they are whiny, tired, hungry, or bored, their behavior is unlikely to be appropriate.

PART THREE

Solutions for Siblings

CHAPTER 6

Fighting Fair

The question isn't whether siblings will fight. They will. It's inevitable. But how they fight, how often, and how they resolve their arguments are the critical issues that parents must face. And in the long run, sibling quarrels can serve as a vital method of learning valuable lessons in listening, negotiation, and compromise.

The Benefits of Sibling Arguments

Sibling arguments may drive parents crazy, but their disputes actually can be a great learning tool. When sisters and brothers argue and then make up, they learn that anger is natural and, even more important, that you can differ with someone you love and the relationship survives the dispute. Furthermore, when children fight fair, they've learned how to use their words, not their fists. That boosts language skills. As kids acquire effective debate skills with their sibs, it's good practice for learning how to stand up for their beliefs and express their needs with friends or others outside the family. Successfully negotiating a settlement with a sibling helps build a child's self-esteem, too.

Why Does It Bother Us?

Even though sibling arguments can have benefits, nobody likes listening to constant squabbling. For many parents, sibling arguments hit a nerve. Hearing our children fight is especially disturbing because of the fears commonly raised by sibling battles.

At Wit's End

"If you have not fought each other, you do not know each other."

—African proverb

Trouble Zone!

Don't overreact to words expressed by young children. In the heat of an argument, they may yell at a sibling, "I hate you!" But that response may be as much a product of limited verbal skills as anything else. The frustration of not being able to adequately express anger may prompt inappropriate remarks. Make it clear, calmly, that such language is not acceptable, acknowledge the child's feelings, and help him to learn how to argue effectively.

Parents sometimes worry that the frequent disagreements signal a deeper problem between their children. They fear that one child may be overwhelmed by his older sibling and develop a tendency to be the victim, at home and outside. Conversely, they are concerned that the more aggressive sibling will become a bully.

Another fear arises when parents dream that their offspring will be lifelong best friends. Will all these fights end that fantasy? Parents are concerned that the angry clashes will damage the sibling relationship permanently.

Surprisingly, the answer is a resounding "yes and no." Siblings don't always grow up to be best friends, but that's not because of their childhood arguments. There are a host of reasons why many siblings remain close as adults. At the same time, childhood battles become the fodder of stories passed down through the generations, usually with a smile. But these disputes rarely affect the adult relationship between siblings.

Why Do They Fight?

Siblings argue for many of the same reasons that most people do, and for a few reasons that are unique to them. Sometimes, brothers and sisters simply disagree with each other. There's no deep, underlying meaning to the dispute. In a fight over a toy, they each may genuinely want the toy—and, in fact, may have equal claims to it. But kids also argue for reasons beyond the subject matter of the argument:

- They may want your attention. Fights often are an effective way of getting parental attention.
- They may not want to share. The bottom line for many fights is wanting something: a toy, the TV remote, the computer, the room, the air they breathe! Frequently they share beautifully, and just as often, they want nothing to do with the concept. So they fight most with the person they have to share with the most—a sibling. They live together, day after day after day. Familiarity breeds contempt—and disputes. Siblings spend a lot of time together. They have to share living space, even if they have separate rooms. They borrow things without asking. Fights happen.

- They disagree on what's fair. Sometimes the arguments are a difference of worldview.
- They are tired, hungry, or bored—maybe all three.
- They are angry with someone else, so they vent it on a safe target—a sibling.
- They are competing for a privilege, toy, grades, and so on and argue over it or something else entirely.
- They fight just because they can!

Stop the Fight Before It Begins

Some disagreements can be avoided. Not all, probably not most. But sometimes, you can avoid situations that provoke fights. Here's how:

- *Be prepared*—The witching hour, right before dinner, is prime time for sibling spats. It's nobody's finest moment, neither for parents nor for kids. This is a good time to preemptively separate youngsters who are overtired, hungry, and cranky. If nothing else, put them at opposite ends of the couch so that they can't touch one another. Give them healthful snacks so that they can last until dinner.
- *Individualize activities*—Sibling rivalry will be milder if the sibs aren't constantly together. Although it simplifies parents' lives if all kids participate in the same activities or share play dates, it fuels competition. Let them pursue their own interests and friends.
- *Make a (peace) schedule*—To avoid conflicts over TV shows, computer privileges, video games, and other major forms of sharing, have the kids help you develop a schedule for these activities. Then there will be no question of whose turn it is.
- *Carve out niches*—If kids have to share a room, it becomes even more important to find private space for each one, even within tight confines. The area is more important than the decor. Even if an attic isn't tall enough for an adult to stand comfortably, it might have a high enough ceiling to be a child's private hideaway. Or an unfinished basement might provide some much-needed respite for warring sibs. In the shared bedroom, rearrange the furniture, hang curtains, or erect a screen so that each child has some privacy.

Did You Know?

According to a study by University of Pittsburgh researchers, boys with the most behavior problems had two things in common. They had abnormally high incidences of sibling conflicts, including kicking, fighting, and yelling. And their mothers tended to respond to their children with criticism, hostility, and physical punishment. Children learn by example, and experts found that boys mimicked with their siblings the hostile behavior exhibited by their mothers.

- *Channel energy elsewhere*—Teach your kids to work off some of their excess energy or pent-up emotions through physical exertion. Biking, swimming, or even pummeling a pop-up toy punching bag can divert some of the energy that might otherwise erupt into a sibling dispute.
- *Factor in downtime*—Youngsters who are overscheduled or overworked are more likely to lose it with their sibs. Make sure there is time for each child to relax, kick back, and enjoy being a kid.

The Parent's Role in Sibling Fights

Walk away. That's the rule of thumb when it comes to how parents should deal with their kids fighting. It's easy to get caught up in the squabbles and to serve as judge, jury, and executioner. But that role is self-defeating. Since many of these fights are a bid to gain parental attention, assuming the role of mediator between the children is counterproductive. Furthermore, if you intervene, you may feel obliged to assign blame, which only fuels the kids' arguments of "You like her best" or "You treat him better" or "You never take my side" or the perennial favorite "You're not fair." Instead, parents can play an active role in teaching their children how to resolve their own conflicts. Here's how parents can help:

- *Play detective*—Figure out the trigger points for most arguments. For a week, keep a log of each sibling spat, and see if you can spot a pattern. Is there a certain time of day when arguments are going to erupt? It might be the hour before dinner, but it could also be the morning, when the household is rushing around to get to school, day care, and job. Do most fights happen before bedtime, when everyone, parents and kids, is overtired? Do they routinely fight over the same thing, such as who controls the remote or who sits in which chair at dinner? If the behavior follows a clear pattern, you have a better chance of making the necessary changes to avoid sibling eruptions.
- *Bring the funny*—Don't be afraid to poke fun at yourself or use humor to defuse a threatened explosion. While humor should never mock

a child, making warring siblings laugh may calm down a situation so that cooler heads can prevail.

- *Catch them when they're good*—Parents need to reinforce good behavior, not merely punish misdeeds. Offer praise when your kids are cooperating or when they've worked out their own compromise.
- *Don't make assumptions*—Parents often presume that the oldest is the instigator of most sibling fights. It may be true that the firstborn will be the one yelling or hitting, but don't assume that the younger sib is blameless. Brothers and sisters early on figure out each other's hot buttons—and push them frequently to spark reactions.
- *Acknowledge their anger*—Kids sometimes have a perfectly legitimate reason to be angry with their sibling. Acknowledge their feelings, and give them permission to feel the whole range of emotions that result from a close relationship. Stress that what's important is the way they resolve the angry feelings.
- *Emphasize your faith in the children*—Tell your children that you believe they can work out their differences on their own. Tell them you trust their judgment, and praise them for their efforts.
- *Model good behavior*—Your children are watching how you handle disagreements. Be sure to show respect and listen when arguing a point with your husband or friends. The adage, "Do as I say, not as I do," rings hollow. Furthermore, if you are constantly angry with your children, that rubs off. If necessary, attend an anger management course to deal with your emotions.
- *Ban violence*—Make it clear that you will not permit any physical violence. The bottom line should be that hitting, kicking, and biting are unacceptable, no matter what the provocation. Any argument that has degenerated into physical violence should be stopped immediately and the combatants separated. The ban on violence must be an ironclad rule. Be on the lookout for emotional or psychological intimidation as well; that's not permissible either. Help the kids find words to express anger so that they don't resort to fists.
- *Be their coach*—Teach your children how to fight fairly. Learning the skills needed to negotiate compromise will be valuable throughout their lives. Work on conflict resolution in peaceful moments, not when the siblings are in the middle of a fight.

Trouble Zone!

For safety's sake, if kids fight in the car, pull over and stop until peace is restored.

Trouble Zone!

What behaviors are you modeling for your children? If parents tend to be competitive and argumentative with each other, that may be seen as acceptable behavior by kids. Take a good look at how the adults in the family interact, and model the behavior you want to see in your children.

- *Remind them of what they know*—If siblings are having trouble resolving an argument, don't just intervene and settle it for them. Instead, review the tools they already know for negotiating a settlement. Start them off, then let them handle the problem themselves.

Settling Disputes Fairly

The same negotiation techniques taught in business schools can be used to teach siblings how to fight fair. Children need to learn how to resolve disputes so that neither side feels like a loser. A win-win solution is always the best resolution. The goal is not to decimate your opponent but to be able to emerge from the negotiations able to work together again. That principle is critical to resolving sibling arguments because siblings do have to live and work together. If one child feels continually as if he is on the short end of the stick, further arguments are much likelier.

There are three basic ways of resolving a conflict:

- *Acquiescence*—One side totally caves to the other side's demands.
- *Compromise*—Both sides yield something after negotiation.
- *Coexistence*—Both sides agree to disagree. Neither side yields, and the issue is not resolved to anyone's satisfaction. Coexistence should only be a last resort.

To help your children learn about negotiating a satisfactory resolution, teach them the following basic rules for fair arguments:

- *Begin statements with* I—Siblings need to learn that when expressing anger, their statements should be specific to their own emotions. "I am angry because . . . ," or "I feel hurt because . . . ," or "I hate it when you. . . ." Children need to speak to their own feelings.
- *Avoid statements that begin with* you—"You" sentences are accusatory, seek blame, and don't further the resolution of an argument: "You are a dork," or "You don't care what I think." Have the child focus on her own emotions and feelings.
- *Skip generalizations*—Statements like "You always sit in my seat" or "I never get a turn" are generally untrue and don't further the discussion. Similarly, exaggerations don't help the situation.

- *Be specific and in the present*—In making an argument, focus on exactly what is the current trouble. Keep the discussion to the issue at hand, and do not revisit past injustices.
- *Don't get personal*—Keep the argument on the issues or on the behavior that is offensive, not on personalities.
- *No name-calling*—Calling names is harmful, inflames passions, and does nothing to resolve the dispute. Avoid belittling your sibling or his concerns.
- *No physical violence*—If kids hit, bite, kick, or engage in any other violence, all conversation ends, and they are immediately separated.
- *No one is a mind reader*—Tell your kids that they need to say what is making them angry, and they must say it in a concise, specific way.
- *Listen carefully*—Tuning out does nothing to resolve a conflict. Kids must listen to what is being said. It's often helpful to have the listener repeat what she believes she's heard to make sure that the two combatants agree on what the issues are. Insist that each child be able to present her side without interruption.

Family Meetings May Help

As your children get older, scheduling regular family meetings may help reduce the number of sibling disputes. This practice delivers a lesson in preventive conflict resolution. The purpose is to discuss family issues, brainstorm for solutions, and negotiate compromises where necessary. Adults and kids learn to work together, as a team, to resolve daily family concerns. When the children are young, parents will need to take a leadership role in the meetings. As the siblings get older, especially in the teen years, they can rotate serving as chairperson of the meetings. The ground rules are simple:

- Each family member's opinion is valued.
- Each person has an opportunity to express her opinion and feelings on a subject but may choose not to talk if she prefers.
- Everyone has to listen.
- No belittling or teasing is permitted.

Great Idea!

When children are trying to work out a resolution to their argument, set a timer for one minute. Have them both marshall their arguments. Then each child should present his side, without interruption, in sixty seconds. It's a short enough time that each child learns to be focused and concise.

CHAPTER 7

Chores and Responsibilities

ouseholds don't run themselves. There's work to be done, and parents can't do it all. Giving kids chores is good for the family and good for them. It teaches them responsibility, builds self-esteem, establishes good habits, creates a good attitude toward work—and, of course, is the source of many complaints. Kids moan about the amount of labor they have to do and about the lack of work, from their point of view, that their siblings are assigned.

Parents should assign each child age-appropriate chores but should also plan some jobs that require the kids to work together. Joint projects may result in more protests, but they build an important sense of teamwork. Plus, joint chores are the stuff of memories. Long after the family car has been assigned to the junk heap, the memories of brothers and sisters washing it and spraying each other with the hose will linger.

What's Reasonable

Kids can start helping around the house almost as soon as they can walk—and maybe even when they can crawl! A toddler can certainly take all the paper napkins from the dinner table and throw them in the trash can. That can be her special job! You will certainly have to help

At Wit's End

"Becoming responsible adults is no longer a matter of whether children hang up their pajamas or put dirty towels in the hamper, but whether they care about themselves and others—and whether they see everyday chores as related to how we treat this planet."

—Eda LeShan,
author, *Kids Are Worth It*

your youngest children do their assigned tasks or at least supervise carefully, but the goal is to make chores a normal part of being in a family.

What kinds of chores are appropriate for kids? Here are some suggestions based on age:

- *For preschoolers*—Fill the pet's food dish or sprinkle food into the aquarium for the fish (carefully show how much to put in, since overfeeding fish can be harmful). Put clothes into the hamper. Empty the clothes from the dryer into a basket. Bring in the mail. Put the newspapers in a recycling bin. Empty wastebaskets. Help put away groceries (for example, boxes of cereal in the cupboard, cans on the shelf). Separate laundry into piles of whites and colors. Put away the bath toys. Stack diapers in the changing table.
- *For ages six to eight*—Sort clean laundry into piles for each member of the family. Match up socks. Set and clear the table. Wipe up spills. Make the bed. Answer the telephone (an eight-year-old child can take messages).
- *For ages nine to eleven*—Change the linens on the beds. Unload the dishwasher. Care for pet (walk, feed, take pet-care jobs in the neighborhood). Rake leaves. Baby-sit younger siblings when adult is home. Carry laundry baskets to the washer, and sort and deliver clothes. (They may need help folding.) Wipe down counters. Wash, dry, and put away dishes (possibly with some help).

Some of these chores are perfect for siblings to do together. The preschooler can empty the dryer; the older sibling can carry the basket upstairs. A preschooler with an older sibling can set the table. Almost all children can carry their own dishes to the sink.

Learning to Do Chores

Besides helping out, chores teach children about organizing and setting priorities. But those lessons are not automatic. Parents need to incorporate household tasks into the lives of their kids, making the work routine and expected. While there may still be complaints, there will also be the understanding that "this is what we do as a family." Here are some ways to succeed:

- *Start early*—Have children help out as early in life as possible. There's no question that in the beginning, their help just makes more work for you. But in the long run, it will pay off for the children, the parent, and the household.
- *Explain what you are doing*—Children acquire language faster when parents talk to them. As you go about your chores or help the older sibling do his chores, explain to the baby what you are doing. Make it as simple as, "Your brother, Dan, is separating the colored clothes into a separate pile from the whites for the wash." Before long, the younger child will be able to do the same chore.
- *Make it fun*—Chores don't have to be, well, chores. You can make a game out of a chore. It can be a contest (who rakes up the biggest pile of leaves?). You can time it (who can put away the most blocks in one minute?). You can put on music and sing along. It helps if the parent is in the same room when the youngster is working, even if the two are doing different tasks. Working in the same room makes the chore quality time with the parent. Some of the best conversations kids have with parents are over the sink doing the dinner dishes! It's amazing how topics spring up when Mom or Dad is washing and the child is drying.
- *Teach priorities*—Make clear that generally work has to be done before play can begin. "We can go build with blocks after we put away the laundry." This statement not only makes it obvious that household chores need to be done, but it also gives an incentive to work together to accomplish the task faster. *Important:* occasionally, you have to forget about chores and share spontaneity with the kids. You're not being irresponsible if you give time off judiciously. Make it clear that you can't ignore the work routinely but sometimes it's OK to say, "It's a beautiful day. Let's go to the park. The chores will wait." Just make sure to do the work upon returning.
- *Organize yourself*—Help your children keep things neat by establishing a place for everything. It helps cleanup when there are open bins and crates for blocks and toys, shelves for books, shoe boxes for

At Wit's End

"But doing the dishes with my mom—when there was nothing 'good' on TV—gave us the opportunity to talk to each other. . . . At times, I have to admit, I even looked forward to doing the dishes. I wasn't big on sharing my feelings, but I often found the experience to be very relaxing and very fulfilling. I often finished the chore feeling much closer to my mother, and that was a feeling that I needed very badly to experience."

—Tom Walsh,
Detroit Free Press columnist

pencils and markers, and so on. For children who can't read, attach a picture of the object that is to be stored in the crate. Avoid closed toy chests, as they can be a safety hazard to young children and toys become jumbled and ignored as they drift to the bottom.

- *Model good behavior*—Clean up after yourself. Establish set places for things like keys, telephone and address books, and reference materials. It's hard to make the argument for a child to clean her room if your bedroom is a mess.

- *Break down the task*—A child, even a ten-year-old, can be overwhelmed by a general order like, "Clean up your room." Breaking down the task into specific chores makes it manageable. "Make your bed, put your dirty clothes in the hamper, empty your trash basket, put the toy cars in the bin, and put the books on the shelves." If the child is young, you may need to give directions one at a time so as not to confuse or overwhelm him. When he has completed one step, you can give him the next task. After going through the process enough times, the child will internalize what needs to be done and won't need the parent to break it up into smaller chunks.

- *Stop the bribery*—Kids have chores because kids are part of the family. When you offer bribes for doing the work that needs to be done to make the household function, you imply there is a choice. "I'll buy you a toy if you set the table." What happens if the child decides she doesn't need the toy and therefore won't set the table? Setting the table should not really be a choice. It's reasonable to pay extra for jobs not normally assigned. For example, if an older child paints the back steps, you might pay her, but for cleaning up her room, no pay is needed.

- *Include everyone*—Assign jobs to stepkids who don't normally live full-time in the house. It's a quiet way to encourage sibling bonds. If nothing else, you will give stepsiblings something in common to gripe about.

- *Offer praise freely*—Yes, kids need to do their jobs, but everyone appreciates a compliment. Notice something specific about how your children completed their tasks. "I like the way you arranged all the stuffed animals on the shelf." Thank each child for helping to make the house run more smoothly. Lavish praise if the siblings have worked well together.

Older Siblings as Baby-Sitters

One of the best ways an older child can help parents is to baby-sit his younger siblings. It's certainly convenient, and the youngster knows the house and is comfortable with the kids. But before you decide to leave an older brother or sister alone at home with the younger siblings, consider the whole situation:

- Age of the child who will be the sitter
- Age(s) of the child(ren) for whom the sitter is responsible
- Personalities and temperaments of the children
- Length of time you will be gone and the distance you'll be from the home
- The children's activities during that time (sleeping, needing a meal, watching TV)

Age Issues

Kids as young as ten can certainly serve as mother's helpers, as long as an adult is around to supervise. The older child is an extra pair of hands and a willing playmate for younger ones. But unless the older child is exceptionally mature, it's best to wait until she is at least thirteen before leaving her alone in the house with younger siblings for any length of time.

It's equally important to consider the age of the children who need supervision. Taking care of an infant has different demands than taking care of a four-year-old. Yes, it's quite possible that the baby will sleep through the entire time—but what if she doesn't? How experienced is the older sibling in changing diapers, feeding a bottle, burping, comforting, or coping with colic?

And while the parents might expect that a four-year-old can be easily entertained by popping a tape in the VCR, what happens if the child is bored and decides to bounce on the couch, falls, and hurts himself? It's not an unlikely scenario. Does a ten-year-old know how to deal with this kind of emergency? Even if the preschooler isn't seriously hurt, will the older sibling know how to offer comfort and dry tears? Or will he become rattled as well?

Of course, it's important to consider how many children are being watched. No matter how mature the fourteen-year-old may be, more

than two kids can be a handful. A potentially more difficult situation may exist if the kids are twins or higher-order multiples. While they may entertain each other, if squabbles break out or one gets hurt, it may be too much to expect a teen sitter to be able to handle it.

Personalities and Temperaments

But it's more than just a question of age. One mother said that she couldn't leave her twelve-year-old daughter to watch the girl's two younger brothers, ages nine and six. The problem was that the two oldest constantly clashed. The mother's solution was to make arrangements for the nine-year-old to have a play date out of the house, and the twelve-year-old would baby-sit the youngest. This arrangement was complicated, but the mother felt more confident that all the kids would be happy and safe.

When considering an older sibling as a sitter, ask yourself if she has the self-confidence and assurance to handle the responsibilities. Also be sure that the younger child will not be deliberately willful or act out when left with the older sib in charge.

Arguments can occur at any time between siblings. Parents need to be clear about the behavior expected from both siblings when left at home alone.

How Long, Where the Parents Are, and What the Kids Are Doing

You also need to consider how long you will be absent from the home and how far away you will be. If the sitter is on the young side and relatively inexperienced, keep the time away short (under an hour), and stay local. You want to be able to get home quickly if necessary.

Review carefully what the kids will be doing. Take the time to set up activities that will keep them quiet, involved, and safe. You still need to review all the safety rules with both the "sitter" and the younger children, but try to have the kids engaged in a quiet activity before you leave the house. While you may not normally permit television or videos in the afternoon, these are good times to make exceptions. Young sitters shouldn't be expected to give baths or make or supervise meals. Unless the sitter can administer CPR, it's probably better that the children don't have snacks, to avoid the possibility of choking.

How Often Should Older Sibs Sit?

It's convenient and it may be free (parents need to decide whether to pay the older child for sitting), but be careful not to overburden your child with baby-sitting responsibilities. There is a difference between requesting, "Watch the kids while I run to the store for milk," and expecting an older child to baby-sit sibs every Saturday night. Unless there are budgetary constraints, offer to hire an outside sitter if you will need someone for several weekends in a row. Your child may decline and say she doesn't mind baby-sitting, but give her the option, indicating that you are not taking her for granted. If you don't, the resentment that builds might adversely affect the child's relationships with parents and her sibs.

It's reasonable for kids to understand that parents need to have a social life outside of the family, but it's also fair to acknowledge that kids want to be with friends as well. Especially for teens, even when no big plans are involved, just hanging out with friends is a social life and important to their development. Use their sitting services judiciously, and avoid the Cinderella syndrome.

Review the Rules

Although your older child is very familiar with the house and the kids, don't assume that he automatically knows how to be a good baby-sitter. There's a difference between being a sibling and being a sitter. So the first time you leave the child in charge, treat the situation as if you had hired a new sitter. Walk through the safety procedures and expectations as completely as you would with an outsider. Here are important points to review:

- Don't leave the child alone in the yard or in the bathtub for even a second. If the phone is ringing, ignore it and let the answering machine pick up. In the house, stay in the same room, unless the child is asleep. Check on the sleeping youngster every half hour.
- Don't give any medicine, not even over-the-counter medications like Tylenol, without permission. Show your older child how to wash and bandage a simple cut.
- To avoid choking hazards, don't feed any child under four years old nuts, popcorn, hard candy, raw carrots, or food that can cause chok-

At Wit's End

"Sibling rivalry is inevitable. The only sure way to avoid it is to have one child."

—Nancy Samalin, parent educator

ing. Food such as hot dogs or grapes should be chopped into small pieces. Drinking any alcohol is never permitted.

- Even if the house is childproofed, make sure the youngsters stay away from stairs, windows, stoves, and electrical outlets. Watch when youngsters are near standing lamps, televisions, and bookshelves because these items can be heavy and topple over.

- Review the rules in case of fire or an emergency. All children should exit the house immediately, go to a neighbor's house, and then call the fire department. Remind the kids not to try to put the fire out or stop to get pets, toys, or anything else. Make sure the sitter understands that even if he believes it's a false alarm, everyone has to get out of the house as quickly as possible.

- Review the list of emergency numbers, including police, fire, poison control, doctor, and emergency contacts. Make sure that you leave information about where you will be (together with a contact number, if possible) and, if you have one, your cell phone number.

- Point out where flashlights are in case of a power failure, and go over the procedures for the alarm system.

- Lock all the doors, and remind the sitter never to open the door to anyone he doesn't know.

- If someone calls, the sitter should never give out your name or telephone number or let the caller know you're away from home. She might say, "Mom can't come to the phone now. May I take a message?" Tell the sitter to keep the phone free so parents can call. You may want to tell the sitter to let all calls go to the answering machine as a way of screening calls. When she hears your voice, she could then pick up.

- Go over basic house rules, such as no jumping on the furniture, which videos may be watched, and general expectations about behavior. Also, even if your children prepare food when you are home, you may prefer that even your older children not cook while you are out of the house.

Stay in Touch

Even if you are going to be local and away for just a short time, call in and check. If possible, carry a cell phone so that your children can reach you easily. If you don't have a cell phone, leave the phone number of each place you will be.

Even though your child may have your cell phone number memorized, be sure to write it down and post it prominently. In the midst of an emergency, she may not remember the number.

Latchkey Kids

The number of children who are latchkey kids is growing. Many of these youngsters are responsible not only for themselves but for younger siblings as well. Asking a child to baby-sit when you leave after setting up everything is different from expecting a child to come home from school each day and assume responsibility for younger siblings' care.

Sometimes children will be alone only a few minutes until a parent arrives home. One mother of two taught in the same district where her family lived, but her sons, ages twelve and ten, attended a different school. While the kids were dismissed at three o'clock, teachers had to stay until three-thirty. Two days a week, the boys went directly to religious school, and one day a week, a housekeeper was home when the boys arrived. For the other two days, the kids were home alone for about a half hour before the mother arrived.

These safety rules will help:

- Make sure that the children are mature enough and ready to assume the responsibility of arriving home alone.
- Establish a contact in the neighborhood who can check on the children if there is a problem. Give this person a spare key.
- Put up a schedule of what the kids should do while they are home alone: homework first, chores next, and then playtime.
- Agree on a telephone check-in for when the kids arrive home.
- Remind them not to tell friends or others that they are home alone. Also, stress that they should never enter the home if the door is ajar, a window is broken, or a stranger is loitering nearby or trying to get them to engage in conversation. Tell them to go to the closest neighbor (or emergency contact) and call the police.
- Remind them to lock the door once inside the house and, if you have one, reactivate the alarm system.
- Review what snacks are to be eaten. Have them practice making those snacks before permitting them to make them on their own.

Did You Know?

Experts estimate that more than five million children spend some time during the week as latchkey kids.

Take the time to periodically review the child-care arrangements, and do it separately with the older child and the younger sibling(s). Make sure that the child who acts as sitter doesn't feel that this responsibility is too difficult or takes all his spare time. Check to see if the younger one feels comfortable with the arrangements. She may be afraid of coming home to a house without an adult present.

Allowances

Some families tie children's allowances to performing chores. Others believe that allowances and chores are separate issues. Either way, families tend to give larger allowances to older children. Most siblings resent the dollar differential, even when they understand that the financial demands on a first-grader are different from those on a sixth-grader.

This situation requires that parents make several decisions about allowances. They must decide whether an allowance is something given or earned. Can it be withheld as punishment? What should it cover? After answering those questions, parents can begin working with each child to determine how much allowance is reasonable.

Given or Earned?

Some families tie allowances to chores, but most experts see the purpose of an allowance as teaching a child money management. "Earning" an allowance by completing chores poses two problems. First, helping out around the house is part of being a family. All family members have to pull their weight. Money is not the incentive. However, that's different from paying for chores that are above and beyond what is normally expected. A second problem with paying for chores is that the chores need to be done whether or not the child feels the pay is worth it. Might he be willing to forgo his two-dollar weekly allowance in exchange for not cleaning up his room? He might be ready to make that decision, but are you able to live with it?

If, in spite of these drawbacks, you choose to tie chores to allowance, you should develop a contract. Put in writing what work is expected and what the allowance will be if chores are completed. Negotiate ahead of

time, so there is no confusion, whether partial payment is permitted if only some of the jobs are done.

What's the Purpose and What Does It Cover?

Giving a child an established amount of money on a regular basis (every week or, for older kids, every month) is useful for many reasons:

- An allowance gives children some independence.
- They discover the value—and necessity—of a savings plan so they can buy something they want or purchase gifts for others.
- They can contribute their own money to charity.
- They learn to make choices. If your son buys the gum, will he have the cash to buy the comic book he wants?
- They gain an appreciation of what things really cost. Can they save enough, or will they have to earn extra money in order to purchase what they want?
- They begin to understand about budgeting in the short and long term.

State clearly what the allowance is to cover. Develop the list together, but make sure it includes an amount for savings (for things they want to buy for themselves, as well as for others), a certain portion for charity, and some to cover weekly expenses. If your children are responsible for entertainment, such as paying for movies or trips to the video arcade, be realistic about the amount those things cost and how often they can go if they are paying. Of course, you can make the distinction that, if the whole family goes to the movies, parents will pay, but it's your child's responsibility to pay for an outing with friends. Write down the list so it's clear.

How Much?

There are several ways to come up with a dollar figure for allowances:

- Figure out how much you are paying currently per week for entertainment, candy, toys, and so forth, and assign that amount to the child. The child is then responsible for covering those costs.

Great Idea!

Even though allowances are limited, encourage your children to donate a small amount of each allowance to charity. They can choose to save it up so they can make a larger donation at one time or even just deposit a few coins into a charity can each week.

Trouble Zone!

Except for unusual circumstances, don't allow kids to borrow ahead on their allowances. They need to learn how to budget. Going into debt, at this early age, is not a good idea, even if the debt is held at Bank o' Mom or Dear Old Dad's S&L.

Great Idea!

Establish a savings tradition. Insist that children put between 5 and 10 percent of their allowance into savings.

- Draw up a list of expenses (including savings and charity), and determine an allowance based on that.
- Offer a dollar for each year of age.
- Survey friends to learn the going rate in the community.

Whatever method you use, be consistent in paying the allowance each week (or monthly, if that is preferred). A monthly schedule teaches long-term planning, but generally kids need to be teens before they're ready for that type of budgeting.

Children may grumble that older siblings are getting higher allowances. Generally, you can explain that it makes sense because older children's expenses are higher.

CHAPTER 8

Schooltime

For a new kindergartner, there can be something very reassuring about knowing his big brother or big sister is in the same building. Separating from parents in the opening days of school may be a little easier if the younger child has been a frequent visitor to the building when picking up older sibs or attending a school function. And he may get some comfort from having a teacher who previously taught an older sibling. Of course, there are advantages and disadvantages of that scenario.

Competition, always an issue for siblings, rears its ugly head again for school-related issues. Grades, sports teams, extracurricular activities—all are fodder for the battle of the siblings. For some children, especially those following in the footsteps of stellar older sibs, there is a fear that, as one child remarked, "I'll always just be Peter's little sister."

Teachers—Help or Hindrance?

A good teacher is more precious than gold. If your older child was lucky enough to get a creative, caring, effective teacher, it makes sense that you would want your younger child to have the same experience. And it might well be a good idea. If you have already established a good relationship with the teacher, she knows and understands the family dynamic, which can be very helpful.

But is there any downside to a child having the same teacher as his sibling? Like most things associated with raising children, the answer is that it depends—on the children, on the teacher, on the grade, on the

Did You Know?

A British study found that children who have one brother or sister do better in school than those in larger families or those without siblings. Oldest children performed the best. Although it might seem that an only child would have the highest scores, researchers found that interacting with other children was an important part of learning. Only children scored lower in math than children with one sibling.

teaching style. Each child has different needs, and one teacher is not likely to fill all of those needs for all children.

School districts have different attitudes toward the issue, so parents need to scope out both the written regulations on class placement and the unofficial, off-the-book rule:

- Some school districts automatically place a younger sibling with a teacher who taught the older brother or sister. This may also occur when teachers, as they do class placements for the following year, recognize a familiar name and request that the child be placed with them.
- In some schools, you may invoke, unofficially, the "I've been down this road before, and I'm not going again" stance. That's code for "This teacher was a disaster for my older child. I've paid my dues. Assign the younger child to another class." It's all off the record, but it's a reasonable request and is usually honored.
- Other school districts will not honor any requests for teacher placement. They also may not consider whether a sibling has had the teacher before.

Before you request a certain teacher or ask that your child *not* be placed in a certain class, consider the following issues:

- *Does your younger child's personality and learning style fit well with that teacher, or will it be a clash from day one?* Even if a teacher is wonderful, he may not be a good match for a particular child. For example, one mother recalls how her quiet son adored his first-grade teacher, who ran a fairly open classroom. The boy was very self-motivated and thrived in an environment that allowed him to move at his own pace among various stations. But his more boisterous younger sister needed a more structured, organized classroom. Although the mother respected the teacher, she requested a different educational experience for her daughter.
- *Is the teacher able to respect each child's strengths without comparing children to their siblings?* Siblings compare themselves enough. They don't need a teacher to be consciously or unconsciously stacking their performances against each other. One family spent a very frustrating

year of their younger son enduring constant comparisons with his overachieving older brother. It was harmful academically, as well as a source of tension between the two brothers.

- *Are you making the request for your convenience or as the best placement for your child?* This is tricky to sort out because the factors that help create a good educational experience include a strong parent-teacher partnership. It's understandable for parents to hope their younger sibling has the same teacher if they have already built a good relationship with that educator. But step back. Make sure it's a good fit for the child.

If you feel that a specific teacher would—or would not—be a good match for a sibling, here are some tips for making the request:

- From talking to other parents, determine the best method to make a request. Does it have to be in writing to the principal, the school psychologist, or counselor? Is a more informal approach effective? Should you speak directly to the teacher you prefer for the following year, the child's current teacher, or someone in administration?
- The problem with putting something in writing is that it's more likely to end up in the permanent record. When well phrased, this can be fine, but it can't be done more than once or twice. A more informal conversation may be equally effective, and there won't be any permanent record. But parents need to check what works in their particular school.
- The request, to be made before class placements are done, can be as simple as, "John so enjoyed his time in your class. We hope Sam gets you, too." It might also be helpful to mention something to the current teacher because the current teachers usually work with the following year's teachers in doing placement.
- Be sure to put the request in educational terms. Generally, it's more productive if you say why you think a child *should* be with a particular teacher rather than why he *should not* be with someone. For example, suppose your older child's experience with a certain second-grade teacher was not successful, and you don't want to repeat that with his younger sibling. You might say, "I know John had Mr. X for second grade, but I'm not sure that would be a good placement

Did You Know?

Parental involvement is critical for a child's success. One study confirmed that boys whose fathers are emotionally close and involved with them are more likely to go to college and get advanced degrees.

for Sam. I'd love to see him in Ms. Y's class because Sam loves science, and Ms. Y shares this enthusiasm." You've made clear your preference, and you've put it in an educational, rather than a personality, context.

If you and the teacher disagree about placement, be honest and open about your reasoning. You may be able to add a perspective that the teacher doesn't have. You may be able to explain other stressors in the home that might augment your argument why a certain placement is important. Of course, the teacher may be able to offer sound reasons for why a different path would be better for your child.

When the Teacher Compares Siblings

If your child complains that the teacher is making frequent references to her sibling—good or bad—ask for a conference. It's inappropriate and unfair to both children. Follow these tips for a productive meeting:

- Before you meet with the teacher, ask your child for details of when the comparisons are made and why.
- Start the conversation on a positive note. You don't want the teacher to feel defensive. Stress that you both are trying to make sure that your child has a good year.

- Phrase your concerns in terms of what you are hearing at home. "Sam sometimes feels bad when you talk about his brother, John." or "Sam worries that you are comparing him to his older brother."
- Listen to the teacher's explanations. She may not have realized she was doing it or may not have appreciated the impact.

If things do not improve, ask for a second meeting, or request a conference with the principal or school psychologist.

When a Different School Is a Good Idea

For most siblings, attending the same school is a given. But there may be occasions when sending them to different schools is worth at least some discussion. In school districts that permit school choice, or for families who have decided that private or parochial school is a better option, the decision to place siblings in the same school may not be automatic. Some school districts have programs in various locations that emphasize art, science, or bilingual education. It's important to consider what works best for each child. But it's equally important to factor in how the family will work as a whole, whichever decision you make.

It's a balancing act. Clearly, for convenience, having the kids in the same school is easier. You get to know the teachers. You can centralize your volunteer efforts and focus your financial contributions. Of course, being in the same place also can offer security and reassurance to the kids. But if the educational environment is inappropriate for your child, it's worth at least a moment to consider whether different schools would be the wisest decision educationally. One girl's parents opted to send their daughter to a private all-girls school because they believed she would thrive in that environment. They put their son in a co-ed (private) school, rather than choosing a single-sex educational experience for him.

Beware the guilt trip! You may decide that one child will benefit, for whatever reason, from attending a private school, while in good conscience, you see no need to enroll his younger sibling, who is having a good educational experience at a public school. This is a perfect example of distinguishing between treating children *fairly* and treating them

Trouble Zone!

Although older siblings are a great resource for insider info on teachers, sometimes the stories can scare a younger sib about to enter the teacher's class. Remind the younger sibling that he is an individual with his own likes and dislikes. He may prefer the way a teacher handles certain situations—even if his big sister didn't!

Trouble Zone!

If you pigeonhole your son as an athlete, he may be less tempted to try an art class. It limits his options before he starts.

the *same*. You should treat all your offspring fairly, which means you consider what is best for each child and act accordingly. Treating each child the same does a disservice to them all because it does not consider each one's specific needs. What's important is not the amount of money that is spent, but that you know what each of your children requires and that you meet the need. If you meet your children's needs, you will reduce sibling rivalry.

Better at . . . Grades? Sports? Writing? Math?

Siblings can turn almost anything into a competition. But the problem with grades is that they are quantifiable and someone else's assessment. So if one child is an exceptionally good student while her sibling is average, it can hurt.

On the one hand, an accomplished sibling can be the gentle push that encourages a younger or older child to try a little harder. One mother recalls the struggles she had with her third son. He was smart. She knew it. But he made little effort in school. Before he started high school, during a discussion about which classes he would take, he was astonished to find out he wouldn't be accepted into the honors classes his older brothers had taken—unless his performance changed dramatically. Maybe it was just a sudden burst of maturity. Certainly it wasn't the constant parental lectures. But when faced with the concept that his brothers could do something that he wouldn't be allowed to do, the boy became a serious student.

But what if there is a significant difference in ability? Without minimizing the importance of doing well in school, it's important to remember that there will always be differences in children's abilities, whether we're talking about academics, sports, or artistic or musical talent. No two kids are alike, not even identical twins. The answer is clear: parents must encourage each child to work up to his potential for his own sake, not in order to compete with a sibling.

Effort should always be more important than grades. The youngster who tries hard and accepts a challenge but only gets a B in the course will probably be more successful in the long run than the child who nabs an A without effort, relying only on natural ability. The work ethic of the first child will prove valuable in life, whereas natural ability will take a person only so far. One British study confirmed what parents have always known: after examining outstanding performances in the arts and sports, experts determined that "opportunities, encouragement, training, motivation, self-confidence and—most of all—practice determine excellence." As professor Michael Howe, a British psychologist, concluded, "Talent is a myth; it is hard work that brings success." As Howe and his colleagues at Exeter University pointed out in their study of outstanding performances in the arts and sports, Mozart was a genius, but he studied for sixteen years before producing his first masterwork.

It's hard for any child, but in some ways there is an added sting if a younger child is the one outshining an older sibling in a particular field, whether it's academics, sports, or friendships. When a child is feeling overwhelmed by a sib's accomplishments, here's what parents must do:

- Recognize each child's accomplishments. Offer praise when a child makes a special effort or for doing something well, whether it's earning an A in spelling or cleaning up her room without being asked. Make the praise specific and realistic. It's better to say, "I liked the way you used colors in your painting," than to offer the more general, "You're the best artist." The child will appreciate that you took the time to notice specifically what she did and will take the praise more seriously.
- Don't minimize anyone's accomplishments. It hurts one sibling and belittles the other if you play down a child's achievements in order to avoid hurting his sib. Brothers and sisters need to learn to accept and celebrate each other's accomplishments. It will fuel sibling rivalry if one child feels ignored in order to spare his sib's feelings.
- Help each child find areas of strength. While you shouldn't pigeonhole any youngster (assigning the academic one to the role of "great student," while the child interested in sports is thought to be the "athlete"), each child can benefit from carving out a niche that interests her and in which she can achieve some success. It's also important to define success as more than achieving A's or scoring touchdowns. Success is enjoying the activity, working hard at it, making a contribution.

Trouble Zone!

If tempers flare when an older sibling (or parent) tries to help a younger brother or sister with homework, surf the Internet for online help.

Helping Each Child Succeed in School

If a youngster is not doing well in school, what can you do? First, parents need to step back and look at the big picture. Are the child's problems at school something new, or has school performance been a concern for a long time? If it has been a concern over several years, talk to the school psychologist and the child's teacher about getting the youngster tested. The child may have an undiagnosed learning disability and need special help. If the child's academic struggles are a recent problem, ask whether something happening at home—a death, divorce, job loss, illness—could be affecting his performance. Be honest with the school, so the teacher and other staff members can help your child during this time of crisis.

Are you too demanding? Think about what you expect from each child and what you value. Are you insisting on perfect grades or that a younger child live up to an older sibling's successes? Is the pressure to succeed too great for this particular child? Is he afraid to try, for fear he will fail? Parental attitudes and values, sometimes unspoken, can influence a child's performance. If necessary, readjust your attitude.

Once parents have reset the course, here are some concrete ways to help all the siblings live up to their potential:

- Talk to the teachers of classes where your child is having problems. They will be able to tell you what areas need work, and to offer additional support before or after school to help your child catch up.
- Keep on top of schoolwork. Review homework assignments daily. Get weekly reports from the teacher on your child's progress until she is again back on track.
- Stop any comparisons. Don't use the more academically successful sibling as a role model. In discussing school, the focus must be on the individual child and his efforts—with no comparisons.
- Get a tutor if necessary. It may be more productive and less threatening if the tutor is someone outside the home. Having an older sibling work with his younger brother or sister on a consistent basis can easily strain the relationship. It blurs the role of sibling to assume the role of teacher. It can also reinforce the less accomplished student's

fears that he can't compete with his sibling. Parents, too, often have trouble being both teacher and parent. If budget constraints limit hiring a tutor, call the high school honor society to see if they have any volunteers who can help. Check at your house of worship or the senior center for volunteers.

Homework Hassles

When children are in elementary school, you may want to set up a homework center in the house where you can supervise your children as they work. The homework center can be at the kitchen or dining room table or in a corner of the living room. Make sure you keep all the necessary supplies close at hand. For example, if the kids are going to work at the kitchen or dining room table, put pencils, markers, paper, scissors, and reference books in a box that you can bring out for them to use. Set a time for homework, and be consistent about it.

If siblings can't work at the table together without squabbling or fooling around, arrange for them to do their homework successively so that each can concentrate.

Walking or Biking to School or the Bus Stop

It may be appropriate to have an older sibling walk a younger sibling to school (or to the bus stop), provided you prepare both children for the experience. The time spent walking can be an opportunity for the siblings to bond, and the experience may give kids a feeling of independence. But parents need to know whether each child is mature enough to handle walking without parental supervision. Some six-year-olds might be ready, and some eight-year-olds are not. If the older child is not comfortable with the responsibility, it's best not to force her.

Requiring children to walk to school with at least one other child is one of the cardinal rules of safety. Some parents want older siblings to walk with their younger brothers and sisters, but before asking an older child to assume that responsibility, here are some considerations.

At Wit's End

"Doing your child's homework is a bit like believing that they can get into shape by watching someone else exercise."

—Lawrence Kutner,
U.S. child psychologist
and author, *Parent and Child*

Great Idea!

Have your children help you draw a map of their walking route to school. Mark on the map dangerous areas (vacant fields or buildings, creeks, blind spots in the road), as well as safe places where the kids could seek refuge.

- Does the older child want the responsibility?
- Is the older child mature enough to follow all the rules of safely walking to school?
- Will the younger sibling respect the older one's authority in the situation? Does the younger child understand the rules of safely walking to school?
- Will it interfere with the older child's friendships to accompany his younger sibling? Will friends distract the older sib? Will they tease the younger child?

If parents believe both children are ready, then it's important to review the safety rules with both kids. Walk the route with both children before permitting them to walk alone. Point out any hazards (creeks, blind spots or curves in the road, alleys, vacant lots, woods). Rehearse how to cross the street if there isn't a crossing guard or a light. Parents should look at the route from the point of view of a child. Review with the children how to handle problems—for example, a stranger approaches them, someone in a car tries to encourage them to come closer, they get lost, or they see a stray dog or an animal acting strangely (rabies). Other safety tips:

- Insist that your children always walk with a buddy, preferably more than one.
- Set a clear location where the children will meet each day after school.
- Agree, and be sure both kids understand, where the younger child will be dropped off at school. In his classroom? At the school entrance? On the playground? Will the older one wait with the younger one?
- Stress the importance of obeying all traffic signals, signs, and crossing guards.
- Review the need for additional caution when it's raining, foggy, or snowing.
- Point out safe houses on the route—homes of family or friends where the children may seek refuge if they are frightened or sick during the walk home.

- Make sure that all the children have an emergency card in their backpack. The card should include the child's home address and phone number, parents' work numbers, and the number of a friend or family member who could be called.
- Teach your children to call 911 in case of an emergency.

If the older sibling is reluctant to assume the responsibility or begins to complain about it, listen carefully. Encourage her to be honest about her feelings. Perhaps she doesn't want to walk her sibling to school every day but would rather go with friends. The responsibility may feel like too much of a burden. One solution may be to establish a schedule that permits her to do both. The older sibling also may be frustrated or worried that the younger child won't listen to her or runs ahead or isn't following the safety rules. Talk to both children, and make it clear that violating safety rules will not be accepted.

Listen to the younger child. Make sure the big brother or sister isn't being too bossy. If the arrangement isn't working out, reconsider your options. It may be that the younger one is not mature enough and still needs adult supervision for getting to school.

Develop a substitute plan if the older child is unable to walk the younger one to school or back because of special circumstances, such as illness or early-morning or after-school activity. If the two walk without other friends, you also need to develop a plan for days when the younger one isn't going to school so that the older sibling is not walking alone.

Emergency Dismissal

Develop a family plan with your children in case classes are dismissed unexpectedly before the end of the school day because of a weather emergency or problem:

- If the school agrees, ask that both children be taken to an agreed-upon classroom so that you (or a designated representative that both children know) can pick them up together.

Great Idea!

Have the siblings role-play various scenarios that might occur when they are walking to school. What will they do if they encounter a stray dog? If they get separated? If they are approached by a stranger?

- If that is not possible, tell the children and the teacher at the beginning of the school year, and repeat again during the year, in what order you will go to the classrooms to get the kids.
- If you feel confident permitting the older sibling to walk the younger one home, make it clear where they are to meet—inside the school. Stress that neither is to leave unless they are together. They should go to the principal's office if they are unsure about the conditions.
- Make sure both children have in their backpacks telephone numbers to reach parents or caregivers, as well as backup emergency contacts.

CHAPTER 9

Boy-Boy, Boy-Girl, Girl-Girl

It shouldn't surprise anyone that families where all the kids are girls tend to be different from all-boy families. You can say that without indulging in any gender stereotypes. It's not that all-girl households consist solely of book-reading, doll-playing, quiet angels while all-boy households thrive on testosterone-driven sports fanatics. Girls play sports, and boys like to read. But there do tend to be differences in the way the households run and the siblings interact. Research confirms what parents have known: all-of-one-kind families differ from those with children of both sexes.

Another unsurprising finding: same-sex siblings tend to relate to one another more than opposite-sex siblings, spending more time together and sharing more interests. This closeness is exaggerated if the family has all girls or all boys. When all the siblings are the same sex, there is a sense of being on a "team." Belonging to this team may reduce the household stress. If all the siblings share similar interests, it's easier to plan family outings and attend kids' events. Parents feel less divided.

But, as psychologist Walter Toman points out in *Family Constellation: Its Effects on Personality and Social Behavior*, "The younger brother of a brother has lived with an older, taller, smarter, stronger, more perfect boy than himself as far back as he can remember." The same concept could be applied to the younger sister of a sister. Siblings make their own comparisons, measuring themselves next to their same-sex sib. If parents make comments comparing the children—"That's just like your sister" or "You're nothing like your brother"—they exacerbate sibling rivalry.

Did You Know?

According to population studies, parents with two children of the same sex are more likely to have a third child than parents with one boy and one girl.

At Wit's End

"My sister was older by three years, and prettier, and things always seemed easier for her. . . . She was vivacious and popular. I was the loner, full of self-doubt and deadly serious in my inch-thick glasses."

—Diane Sawyer, reporter

"I get my drive from being the second child and a fat child. My sister was smarter and better than I was in every way."

—Joan Rivers, entertainer

Sometimes the parent of the opposite sex feels left out or not quite as competent. That parent worries about not fitting into family activities as well. The mother of a family of boys was told, upon delivering her third son, "Now you'll have to be a jock." Similarly, the father of three daughters wondered if he was up to the task of Brownies and dolls.

The answer for all parents is that we learn to enjoy our children's interests and delight in their accomplishments. Kids share many of the same emotions and require much of the same care, regardless of gender. And it's critical for kids to spend time with the parent of the opposite sex. That gives them a more realistic perspective on the world and makes them more comfortable with the opposite sex.

When raising same-sex siblings, parents must confront some important don'ts:

- Don't gender-stereotype your children. Girls like to go to sports events, and boys enjoy cooking. There's enough categorizing in the media and popular culture. In your own home, encourage children to pursue their interests, regardless of whether it's a typical "boy" or "girl" activity.
- Don't clump your children together. There's a tendency to think of same-sex children as "the boys" or "the girls," as if they were interchangeable. Even if they share many of the same interests, your children are distinct individuals. And remember that one-on-one time is still essential.
- Don't make assumptions based on your experiences. Just because an approach worked with one child, don't expect it to necessarily be effective for the sibling.
- Don't pigeonhole siblings. This is true whether they are same-sex siblings or of the opposite sex. Don't make one the student and one the athlete, or one "emotional" and one "practical." These categories are limiting and may not even be true.

Girl Power

Stereotypes aside, research confirms that girls tend to imitate their mothers and take on a maternal role toward younger siblings, although not initially. When an older sibling is confronted with a new baby, her nurturing instincts generally take about eight months to kick in. This is especially true if the girl has been very close to her mother.

Sisters tend to interact differently with each other than brothers do. All-girl households tend to be quieter. The competition is less overt—but don't think it's not there. Girls tend to be less physically aggressive. But remember, these are generalizations. Your daughters may be loud, competitive, and aggressive. That's fine, too.

One of the advantages of an all-girl family is parental expectations. Parents without sons are more likely to encourage their daughters to study math, science, and other areas of traditionally male expertise. Girls without brothers tend to become more assertive and show leadership potential. Clearly, if you have a family with opposite-sex siblings, it's important that your expectations for academic achievement be based on true ability. You want every child to live up to his or her potential, regardless of gender.

According to a recent study by the American Association of University Women, "Girls, when compared to boys, are at a significant disadvantage as technology is increasingly incorporated into the classroom. Girls tend to come to the classroom with less exposure to computers and believe that they are less adept at using technology than boys. While boys take advanced programming classes, girls take data entry, and only 17 percent of Advanced Placement test takers in computer science are girls."

Great Idea!

Arrange opportunities for daughters raised in all-girl households to interact with the opposite sex by joining mixed-gender teams or playing with neighborhood boys or male cousins. Parents of all-boy households also should deliberately seek times when their sons can play with girls. It will reduce their discomfort around members of the opposite sex.

Boys Will Be Boys?

The all-male household tends to be louder and more physically aggressive. Brothers also tend to engage in more competitive activities. In fact, at times it seems as though every activity can be reduced to an "I win, you lose" event. But don't assume that because you literally have to pry them apart from each other during another wrestling match on the floor, they aren't close and don't love one another. Boys tend to develop impulse control later than girls. Nor do these childhood brawls portend a poor adult relationship. Research has shown just the opposite. Brothers are expressing a wide spectrum of emotions, including love and caring, in their boyhood fights. But again, these are broad generalizations.

At Wit's End

"I see nothing wrong with giving Robert some legal experience as Attorney General before he goes out to practice law."

—President John F. Kennedy, on his appointment of his brother

Not every all-boy household appears to be a set for the World Wrestling Federation.

As with girls, stereotypes continue to abound, but recent studies have disproved the assumption that boys are less emotional than girls. Researchers who tested second-grade boys and girls found that boys were more emotionally stressed when listening to a crying baby but were less capable of handling the emotions than girls. In response, boys try to avoid the situations of emotional conflict. In another study, researchers found that parents responding to a child's question about emotions are likely to give a longer explanation to a daughter than to a son. The parents also are more likely to ask a daughter to speculate on the feelings behind the emotion. Furthermore, researchers have found that even in preschool, girls' vocabularies include more words about emotions, like *love*, *sad*, *angry*, and they use these words more often than boys do. Encourage your sons to express their emotions. Model this behavior by using words to describe your feelings.

Boy-Girl Households

When boys grow up with sisters and girls live with brothers, they develop an ease and comfort with the opposite sex. It's one of the advantages of the boy-girl sibling household. These children view the opposite sex with more realistic eyes. They are more likely to have friends of both genders.

Without resorting to gender stereotypes, access to toys generally assigned to the opposite sex broadens the worldview of the younger sibling. For the younger sister of an older brother, toys available at home usually include the trucks, action figures, and sports equipment typically given to boys. The exposure to what are considered "male" toys is healthy. Similarly, the younger brother of an older sister tends to be comfortable around dolls and all the other paraphernalia people tend to buy for girls. The brother can play with a dollhouse as easily as his sister.

A challenge of boy-girl households is that parents can intensify sibling rivalry between brothers and sisters if they divide their focus based on gender. Resentment grows if the mother spends more one-on-one time with the daughter while the father concentrates on the son. That's harmful. Spending time with the parent of the opposite sex is vital to the

development and maturity of each child. Nor do you want to assign chores based on gender. Girls can mow lawns, and boys can baby-sit.

Let family outings reflect the interests of all members. Don't assume that a girl won't enjoy a football game or that a boy won't enjoy the ballet. It's important that your son and daughter understand that your expectations and dreams for them aren't limited by gender.

This isn't always easy. An Arizona State University study reveals that children believe others will be more likely to approve of their behavior if they play with same-sex peers than with opposite-sex peers.

Whatever the composition of your family, remember that each child is an individual, with his or her own personality, strengths, preferences, and fears. Don't let the family makeup lead you to make assumptions about behavior or influence how you interact with each child.

Did You Know?

Boys outnumber girls about three to one in computer science classes, and almost two to one in physics.

CHAPTER 10

Special Circumstances

Multiples and Siblings with Special Needs

*S*ibling relationships are naturally complex. But there are certain circumstances that add another layer to the dynamic. These special circumstances can include multiple births, as well as siblings who have special needs, such as a physical, intellectual, emotional, or psychological disability.

Twins, triplets, and higher-order multiples relate to each other as siblings, but being a multiple has its own psychological and emotional implications. In addition, being the older or younger sibling of a set of twins or triplets is not quite the same as being the brother or sister of a singleton. For simplicity, the discussion of multiples in this chapter will focus on issues concerning twins. Twins will also be used in the examples. Families with higher-order multiples—triplets, quadruplets, or higher—face the same problems but to a greater degree because of the additional children.

Sibling relationships are also seriously affected when one of the children has a chronic disease or is emotionally, intellectually, or physically disabled. These special circumstances will influence how the siblings interact. The presence of the special-needs sibling and the nature of the family's response will also influence the nondisabled youngster's view of himself, his role in the family, his relationship with his parents, and his daily life in general.

More than One

Twins (or higher-order multiples) have never known what it's like to be an only child. Even if their births were the first in the family, they've always had a sibling. While everyone assumes that multiples will be close, the potential for sibling rivalry is in some ways increased because comparisons are inevitable. Because twins are the same age and, in the case of identical twins, have a similar appearance, outsiders as well as family members are quick to measure one child against the other. As soon as one twin walks, the question becomes, Why isn't her twin walking, too? People are more likely to see each sibling as an individual when there is a year or more between their ages. When the kids are the same age, it's hard to avoid comparisons. Even so, parents must.

Unfortunately, one way parents sometimes avoid comparisons is to pigeonhole their children so that each one is known for something special. One mother of triplets said she caught herself labeling one of her six-year-old daughters as artistic, her other daughter as an exceptional gymnast, and her son as an outstanding athlete. But she laughed and added, "Even if the artist isn't as good at cartwheels, [it] doesn't mean she can't enjoy them and we shouldn't cheer for her when she tries— just like we hang up the pictures of all the kids, whether they seem to exhibit artistic talent or not." Putting labels on kids can put limits on their potential. It also fails to eliminate sibling rivalry. For some children, those labels may encourage them to rebel and resist the typecasting.

A Gentle Push

From birth (perhaps even in utero), twins learn from each other. Even as babies, when cooperative play is several years off, twins watch and mimic each other. It's one of the reasons that many develop "twinspeak," that special language only they can understand. Having a twin helps at each developmental stage. It motivates the children, gently pushing each one to keep up with the other. Carefully watching each other, they spur each other on.

Because twins are the same age, parents assume they will be at the same developmental level. But as with any two individuals, their development can vary and it's not unusual for them to arrive at various milestones at different times. Rather than setting one twin's behavior as the norm for measuring the sibling, parents find it helpful to recognize the range of what is normal for children at each developmental stage. For example, babies usually take their first steps when they are somewhere between twelve and fifteen months old. Some infants start walking before they are ten months old, while others are content to crawl until they are eighteen months old. The range for what is normal is broad. Therefore, rather than compare their twins' developmental milestones to each other, parents should see how each child is doing against the norm for all children of that age. Furthermore, multiples are at greater risk for being born prematurely. For children born early, development must be judged by different standards. Talk to your health care provider if you have any concerns.

Avoiding comparisons between your multiples is critical. These comparisons encourage children to measure themselves against each other— and always come up short. It's one of the most common roots of sibling rivalry.

At Wit's End

"Twins are at the same place psychologically and developmentally, so their relationship is fraught with more competition because of their intense desire to have the same things, from parental attention to the toys they play with."

—Jane Greer, Ph.D., author of *Adult Sibling Rivalry*

Socialization Skills

Whether or not they converse in twinspeak, twins are generally more socialized than most firstborns or only children. They are rarely lonely or in need of peer companionship. Of course, the downside of this built-in play date is that they may not be as able to entertain themselves when either one is alone.

Parents should deliberately make an effort to have one-on-one time with each twin, not plan all activities to include both. This will reduce sibling rivalry, as each child has time alone to interact with a parent. It will reinforce each child's sense of individuality, so critical to self-esteem.

Even though it's more trouble for parents, at times it is important to plan separate play dates for the twins, so each one has an opportunity to make outside friends. Again, this experience strengthens each child's sense of self and reinforces that she is not merely an extension of her twin. But this kind of individual attention takes planning. Here are some tips:

- Arrange at least two different activities, preferably in separate rooms. Rotate the pairs of twin and friend between the activities.
- At times, arrange for one twin to go on a play date outside the home while the other twin invites a friend for the afternoon.
- Limit the play date to about an hour if both twins are home with friends.
- Be available. Even if your goal is to encourage each twin to play one-on-one with his friend, it's quite possible that the whole group will want to play together at some point. Monitor this closely so that no child feels left out.

The Art of the Deal

One of the important by-products of being a twin is that children learn early the art of the deal. They acquire sharp negotiating skills because they are peers and the balance of power is even, unlike that between an older sibling and a younger brother or sister. That's not to suggest that there aren't plenty of times that twins fight over toys. They fight as much, if not more, than their singleton siblings. And because they are together so much, they quickly understand exactly what buttons to push to provoke a reaction.

Twins' fights generally involve two equal opponents, in contrast to the arguments between siblings of differing ages. But the parental rules are the same (see Chapter 6 for more tips on sibling fights). Remember these principles of fair arguments:

- Aggressive behavior, including hitting, kicking, and biting, is always unacceptable.
- Let the siblings work it out themselves without parental interference unless real physical or emotional harm is being done.
- Don't try to figure out who started the argument. It doesn't matter.
- Send the siblings to separate rooms if they can't resolve the dispute themselves. Separation prompts boredom, which generally results in a resolved dispute.

Don't try to eliminate sibling rivalry totally. It can't be done, and it wouldn't be healthy if it could. Kids learn important, lifelong lessons from disputes that they settle themselves.

Multiples and Their Singleton Siblings

It's not easy being the singleton sibling of a set of twins (or higher-order multiples). It's easy to get overlooked. One mother of triplets described how awkward it was when she would go out with her six-year-old daughter and the newborn triplets. "People would make a fuss over the babies and ignore their big sister. On the one hand, she was old enough to be able to talk about her feelings. On the other hand, she had been an only child for many years, and it would have been an adjustment to have had a single sibling, let alone three in one fell swoop."

Here's how to make sure that singletons don't get overshadowed by their twin siblings:

- Be sure to make time for one-on-one interactions with the singleton. She needs the personal parental attention.
- Talk to your singleton about his feelings, and give him the opportunity to voice his frustrations.
- Encourage the singleton to build individual relationships with the twin siblings and interact with each child separately.

Trouble Zone!

Calling children "the twins" reinforces the concept that they are a single unit. To encourage individuality, when referring to multiples, use their individual names.

Birthday Celebrations

Birthdays are special for any child. It's an opportunity to celebrate and rejoice in your youngster's life. That's why it's especially important for parents of multiples, no matter how they choose to mark the occasion, to emphasize the individual nature of the day. Referring to the children by name makes the point. For example, you might say, "Let's talk about the party for John and Steve's birthday." That's different from "Let's talk about the twins' birthday." The first emphasizes the individual nature of the celebration; the second suggests the children are a single unit. It may be a matter of semantics, but it's an important distinction.

Gifts for birthdays and holidays should be selected to appropriately reflect each child's interests. Parents may opt for one large gift that the twins will share—for example, a train set—but it's also important that twins receive at least one small present individually selected for them. These gifts don't have to be expensive, but they should be thoughtful. If you want to give books, for example, make sure that the subject matter is something that each child finds interesting. Again, the message you want each twin to hear is, "You are individuals, even if you share a birthday."

Some families choose to have separate parties for each twin. The parties can be on the same day, successive days, or successive weekends. Another alternative is to sponsor a "half birthday" celebration. One twin has a party on the actual birth date; the other, six months later.

Other families opt to individualize the activities within a single celebration. It may be less expensive to have a single party, especially if you are using professional party services, such as a clown or magician. There's probably no extra charge for honoring two children at the same party, although there may be a nominal fee for the extra commemorative gift (for example, a T-shirt or banner) if the guest of honor receives something from the entertainer. Either method works, but as the twins get old enough to express their opinions, it's important to include them in the discussion of how they want to celebrate their birthdays.

Here are some tips for personalizing a joint party:

- The rule of thumb for any child's birthday party, especially when children are young, is to invite one guest for each year of age. That translates to three guests if the birthday child is turning three. Even parents of singletons frequently have problems adhering to this rule! If at all possible, permit each twin to choose a few children he wants to invite, as opposed to developing a single guest list. There will probably be overlaps, but each twin will appreciate the effort to make up his own guest list. That said, it really will simplify the party if you can limit the number of guests as much as possible.

- With a larger guest list, arrange for more adult supervision.
- As the children get older, let them plan most of the party's activities, decorations, and refreshments. If budget permits, allow each child to choose his own decorations. They don't have to match or even be compatible.
- If you can afford two cakes, it's a small but significant gesture that emphasizes the individual nature of the occasion. Especially for younger children, an even better alternative is to serve individual cupcakes for hosts and guests alike. A nice touch—with no extra cost— is to sing two rounds of "Happy Birthday," personalized for each child.

While it would be lovely if party guests brought appropriate gifts for each twin, that may be too much of a demand on another family's budget. Instead, guests might bring a gift that the twins can share. That's why it's especially nice if parents of the multiples recognize each child with individual presents.

School Issues

Parents of multiples may not have any choice in whether their twins can be in the same classroom. Some school districts insist upon separating multiples as early as kindergarten. But in preschool, a strong argument can be made for keeping twins together in the same classroom, for the children's sake as well as for the parents' convenience.

Twins draw great strength and security from being together. While some people worry that twins won't separate enough to interact with other classmates, in fact, that's frequently not the case at all. Having the security of each other gives them the confidence to socialize and interact with other children.

Once twins get into elementary school, there are pros and cons of keeping them in the same classroom. According to a survey by the

Great Idea!

Party decorations don't have to match if it's a joint birthday party for twins. Choose a plain tablecloth, and put individualized decorations on the table that reflect each twin's interests. For example, for the twin who wants a space theme, the centerpiece might be a spaceship. Next to it might be footballs and baseballs for the twin who loves sports.

National Organization of Mothers of Twins Clubs, 43 percent of educators believe twins should be placed in separate classrooms beginning in kindergarten. But others disagree. Keeping twins together in the same classroom provides several advantages:

- The social support twins derive from each other can encourage independence, while separation, especially when the children are just beginning school, may be traumatic.
- It would be counterproductive if separating twins were the criterion for placement in a specific class, rather than trying to match teaching style to student.
- Parents may find it more convenient to have the twins in the same classroom for volunteer purposes, back-to-school meetings, teacher conferences, reviewing homework, and other forms of parental involvement.

Placing twins in separate classrooms also can have benefits:

- It may reduce the inevitable comparisons between the twins by teachers, classmates, and themselves.
- It may cut down on the competition between the twins. To a certain extent, competition can spur achievement, but it can also detract from the purposes of education, changing the focus from learning to being better than the other twin.
- Having twins in the same classroom may distract from the learning process. Twins draw attention just because they are unusual (and higher-order multiples draw even more attention). It may change the social dynamic in the classroom if they play exclusively with each other.
- It may be unfair to other children, who don't have the social support of having a sibling in the classroom.
- Separating twins may encourage them to develop their individuality and independence.

If parents feel strongly that the twins either need to be together or need to be separated, they should discuss their concerns with the school's teachers, administrators, and counselors. Before meeting with school personnel, however, you need to do your homework so that you come prepared:

- Talk to other parents of multiples—especially those whose children are or have been in the same school—about their experiences in separating or keeping twins together. Ask them what factors made the difference in their decision.
- Talk to your twins' preschool teachers to get a clear idea of how the twins behaved in the classroom. Were they able to separate? Did they play independently? Did they form friendships with other children? Did they exclude others?
- Talk to your children, and see if they have a preference—and why. But talk to each one separately so that one doesn't feel intimidated by the other's choices. While you may not be able to honor their wishes, you need to know what they want. When you need to explain the final decision, it will help if you can speak about their concerns and give reassurance.
- Trust your own judgment. After listening to experts, other parents of multiples, and your children, think about what you know about your children and what you believe would be in each one's best interests.
- Be flexible. Whatever decision is made, you may need to reconsider it if circumstances change.

Siblings with a Chronic Illness or Disability

The sibling relationship between a child and a brother or sister with a chronic illness or disability can be very similar to that of a youngster with a nondisabled sibling. Despite the problems, the siblings do share the same parents and a family history. Depending on the nature and severity of the illness or disability and the way it's handled within the family, there can be long-term effects on the sibling relationship.

It's also clear that living in a family with a sick or disabled child will affect the healthy sibling and his worldview, relationship with parents, expectations for himself, and concerns for the future. But research has also shown benefits to children who live in families with a child who is

Did You Know?

More than 5.8 million children in the United States have disabilities. Most of them have brothers or sisters.

Sometimes the nondisabled child is asked to give updates or explain the medical condition of her sibling. Prepare her by giving information, in age-appropriate language, so that if asked, she will be able to give some answer. Depending on her age, she doesn't need extensive details, but for example, if her sibling has cerebral palsy, the explanation might be, "My brother has a disease that makes it hard for him to walk. He gets physical therapy to help him."

sick or disabled. These youngsters tend to be more mature, responsible, self-confident, independent, patient, charitable, and sensitive to humanitarian efforts and to have a greater sense of closeness to the family.

Sibling Concerns

Being the sibling of a child with a chronic illness or disability can give rise to some serious practical and emotional reactions. It's critical for parents to address these fears and concerns openly. It's not a one-time discussion but instead will resurface again and again. Here's what many kids worry about:

- Siblings may feel the need to excel in order to make up for the disabled sibling's problems. Or they may feel guilty because they do excel. Reassure them that you only want each of them to be themselves. Your children don't have to succeed for anyone but themselves, and they should never be embarrassed because they excel in areas where a disabled sibling can't.

- Family activities are sometimes canceled or curtailed because of the sick or disabled sibling's issues. Schedule family activities that all children can enjoy on some level, and schedule time alone with each child.

- Nondisabled children may feel guilty about being normal, worry about all the negative emotions they have about their sibling, and may even feel they are to blame somehow for their sibling's problems. Make sure your child understands he's not responsible for his sibling's disability. Acknowledge his sadness and anger. Reassure him he's not a "bad person" for feeling this way. Help him find a support group or professional help if he is having trouble dealing with his emotions.

- The nondisabled siblings may be embarrassed about their brother or sister's behavior or appearance. Help them understand the reasons for a sibling's appearance or behavior. Reassure them that all emotions are legitimate, but they can't use words to hurt their sibling, even if they are having difficulty dealing with the problem.

- They might worry that they will get sick, too, or that they will develop a disability. In age-appropriate language, explain the disability or illness, and offer reassurances that it's not contagious.

- They might resent the amount of parental attention the disabled child gets. Assure them that it's reasonable to resent the amount of time you have to spend taking care of their sibling, but make time for each of them as well. Enlist outside help or extended family to help with the children.
- The nondisabled children may feel isolated and convinced that none of their peers can understand what it's like to live with a sibling who is sick or disabled. Have them join a sibling support group to reduce their feelings of isolation. Help them find the right words to explain their sibling's condition to their friends.
- Nondisabled siblings may resent the extra chores or caregiving they have to do because of their sibling. Make sure that you remember they are also children, and give age-appropriate responsibilities.

What Parents Can Do to Help

One of the most important ways to help your family cope with a chronically ill or disabled child is to come to terms with the situation yourself. Only when the adults in the family have confronted their family's reality and dealt with their own emotions can they help their children. If necessary, seek outside professional counseling. Support groups for parents (and separate ones for children) can be lifelines. They also lessen the sense of isolation that parents and children facing these issues often confront.

Communication is always very important in families, but it takes on added significance when one of the siblings is ill or disabled. Sometimes, in a misguided attempt to protect the nondisabled child, parents withhold information. But not knowing can be scarier than the truth. In terms that are age appropriate, talk to your child about the sibling's disabilities, how they affect him, and what can be done. Acknowledge the child's feelings and give him permission to have negative feelings about his sibling's situation. It's critical to make the distinction that the situation may be unfair and frustrating, but it's not anyone's fault—not his, not his siblings', not his parents'. Reassure him that you too sometimes resent the situation, but it doesn't mean you love any of your children less.

Here are some other ways you can help encourage a strong sibling relationship:

Great Idea!

Support groups help ease the loneliness and isolation felt when confronted with the pressures of caring for a disabled or chronically ill child. Make sure that nondisabled siblings have the opportunity to meet other kids facing similar situations. Sibling therapy groups provide a nonjudgmental, supportive environment that helps children deal with the emotions they experience having a disabled or sick brother or sister.

- Remember that the nondisabled child is a child, not another adult caretaker. Keep in mind what is age appropriate in terms of chores and responsibilities.
- Watch for signs or clues that the nondisabled child is being bullied or teased at school. Talk about why children say unkind things, and give her the words, if necessary, to explain her sibling's problems.
- Make time for the nondisabled child. It's easy to get overwhelmed by the demands of a sick child, but carve out some one-on-one time with your healthy offspring as well. Consider getting respite care for the disabled child, if necessary, for special events in her sibling's life.
- Talk about feelings of embarrassment. A child may be embarrassed by a disabled sibling's behavior. Give him permission to have angry feelings, but stress that sometimes nondisabled relatives, like parents, can also be embarrassing.
- Keep a sense of humor.

CHAPTER 11

Stepsiblings

The first thing to remember about stepsiblings is that they are kids. It's tempting to read the issue of stepfamily into every situation, but that would be a mistake. While you shouldn't underestimate the impact of being a child in a stepfamily, you shouldn't automatically assume that the family structure is what is motivating the children's behavior. No matter how the family was created, kids argue, are jealous, exhibit pettiness. Some of those behaviors are just the product of living with people and are often a result of kids being kids. If one or all of the stepsiblings are teenagers, you also have to factor normal adolescent craziness into the equation.

A stepfamily where each parent has a set of children from a previous marriage is called a blended or combined family. This situation involves a different dynamic than you find in stepfamily configurations where the stepparent has no children of his or her own. Forming a blended family introduces a whole host of issues. Kids need time to adjust to a new stepparent. If you factor in that the stepparent has children of his or her own, then the stepsibling dynamic is added onto the stepparent-stepchild relationship.

What Are the Issues?

One critical factor is quite simple: blending families often results in less space for more people. Unless money is no object, the size of the house-

Did You Know?

A 1994 study estimates that in the United States, half of the sixty million children under the age of thirteen live with one biological parent and that parent's partner. Among American teens, 35 percent are in stepfamilies.

By 2010 there will be more stepfamilies in the United States than any other kind.

hold increases but not the size of the house! Space may be at a premium during a time when everyone needs more privacy.

Things get tougher when you consider the many differences that can be introduced by stepparents and stepsiblings. The issues may relate to mixing different ages, genders, and most critically, lifestyles and parenting approaches.

Money—or the increased demands on it—frequently complicates the problems. With more children to feed, clothe, and house, finances might be stretched thin.

Then factor in the birth order question. When you combine families, the kids' places may change. Has the oldest child in the family suddenly been supplanted by a stepsib who is older? Has the baby of the family lost his favored spot to a new interloper? With the remarriage of a parent, did the baby of one family find himself the middle child of the newly configured one? Has the only child become one of a group, whether she wanted to or not? Part of the problem stepsibs face is that no one is sure of his or her place in the family anymore.

Time or, more precisely, lack of it also creates friction. If much of sibling rivalry in families can be traced to the children wanting parental attention, the issue intensifies among stepsiblings. Now the kids are not only competing with each other for the birth parent's attention, but they are vying for that attention with new kids who aren't even related to them. Plus the parents, in the throes of a new romantic relationship, may be spending less time with the children.

Then there are the outsiders—the other parent of each child—who may have an opinion on the remarriage, the new stepparent, and the stepsibs. Extended-family members also can add to the tension. How will grandparents treat the new stepgrandchildren? If the treatment is overtly unbalanced, then resentment can build among the stepsibs.

If you are blending his kids, her kids, and adding in a new baby, it's a recipe for hard work and conflict. Kids are being asked to accept not only a new adult in their lives but new youngsters as well. These are complex, difficult concerns that demand a lot from all the parties.

Anyone who is in a combined family knows that the Brady Bunch concept is not only ridiculous but harmful. Even nonblended families don't behave the way that sitcom group did—and certainly it was an unrealistic portrayal of a stepfamily.

Stepsibling Configurations

Blended or combined families include several common forms:

- Father, his children, stepmother without children of her own
- Mother, her children, stepfather without children of his own
- Father, mother, his kids, her kids
- Father, mother, his kids, her kids, their kids
- Stepfamilies where all the children live in the same home
- Stepfamilies where one set of kids lives full-time in the home and the other set visits regularly
- Stepfamilies where one set of kids lives full-time in the home and the other set visits irregularly or infrequently
- Stepfamilies where both sets of kids do not live in the home full-time but visit

There are other variations, and each difference may affect the way siblings interact and how they relate to one another. But most important, the sibling relationship must be viewed in light of how the child is adjusting to the stepparent. That's the critical piece of the dynamic. If there are serious problems between the stepchild and stepparent, then the problems are going to carry over into the relationship between the stepsibs.

What's Reasonable?

Are stepsibs supposed to love one another? Not necessarily. In fact, that's highly unlikely, certainly in the beginning. The parents are in love, but the kids may barely be "in like," if that. And that makes sense. In some cases, the kids may not know each other particularly well before the two families are joined.

Experts recommend moving slowly and allowing all parties, adults and kids, to get to know one another before marriage. But even if that happens, there's no guarantee that the children will like each other. They wouldn't necessarily choose one another for friends, let alone relatives. And because they don't share a history, they need to build a relationship.

What is reasonable? Tell the children that they don't have to like one another, but they do have to treat one another with respect and courtesy.

Encourage kids to see the benefits of a bigger family and the stability and richness of parents who love one another and are committed to each other and to the children—all of them. Choose family activities that deemphasize competition among the stepsibs. Instead, look for things to do as a family that build you as a team. Assign chores that require teamwork, like cleaning the basement together.

Equity Issues

In the Cinderella story, the issue isn't really whether the stepmother loves her own two daughters better than her stepdaughter. It's how she treats the three girls.

Siblings who share parents complain frequently that Mom or Dad loves the other one best. It's a standard refrain intended to push the guilt buttons. But in the case of stepsibs, in fact, it's probably true. Each parent probably does love his or her own children best. That's to be expected. The bigger issue is equity or fairness.

Fair does not mean the *same*. The words don't mean the same thing for siblings who are related, and they don't mean the same thing for stepsibs either. All parents—and that includes stepparents—need to see and treat each child in the family as an individual, responding to the child's particular needs. Here's how parents and stepparents can be fair:

- All kids get responsibilities and privileges based on age and behavior, not based on relationship.
- Chores are assigned to all kids, whether they live in the house full-time or not.
- Expectations for behavior are the same for each age-group.
- Gifts for the kids are given from the stepparents as a couple, not from the individual parent. Parents do not give duplicate gifts just to appear fair. Rather, they select presents that are appropriate for each child's age and interests.

If stepparents are not treating each child fairly and with respect, then sibling rivalry and arguments will undoubtedly increase.

Communication Is the Key

If talking regularly, openly, and honestly is critical in any family, it takes on an added dimension of importance in combined families. At the same time, it's complicated because the participants in these conversations don't necessarily feel comfortable or sure enough about the relationships to be forthcoming. In spite of the challenges, it's up to the adults—parents and stepparents—to encourage stepsibs to talk to each other. Here's how:

Trouble Zone!

Becoming a stepparent is a tough job. It works best when the adults support each other and acknowledge the difficulty—and rewards—of the task.

- Discuss how the kids are going to refer to each other. The prefix *step-* is not pejorative. The kids shouldn't be embarrassed if they refer to each other as stepbrother or stepsister. It is a realistic reference to how they are related. On the other hand, if they prefer to drop the *step*, that's OK, too. The choice of words probably will depend somewhat on the kids' ages when the two families combined. What is not acceptable is to ridicule or make up disparaging names for stepsibs.
- Just like siblings who share parents, stepsibs need to work out disputes by themselves. Stay out of most sibling arguments unless there is some danger to one of the kids. That danger doesn't have to be a physical risk; *repeated* severe emotional distress also is a reason to intervene.
- Teach stepsibs to acknowledge each other's feelings. Encourage them to see the disagreement from the other person's point of view—an important lesson that has lifelong benefits.
- An important component of communication is *listening* to each other. Make sure stepsibs understand that they must be open to hearing the other person's point of view. It's not enough to keep quiet while the other person is talking. Active listening is also required.

Living Arrangements

Sharing rooms can create a host of problems among siblings (see Chapter 3). These issues may take on a more complicated emotional component when the roommates are stepsiblings. Feelings of jealousy and envy, as well as the need for privacy, are often more intense between stepsibs.

Let's look at some of the issues that are likely to arise when a blended family is planning living arrangements:

- *Should a child who is used to having his own room, or was sharing with a biological sibling, now share with a stepsib?* Both kids may bitterly resent being asked to give up their privacy to share with a "stranger," albeit one who is now part of the family. Consider other alternatives, but if necessary, stress that everyone is making a fresh start with the marriage.
- *Does a child who visits infrequently or irregularly need her own room?* Ideally, yes, but if space is limited, it doesn't make much sense to ask children who live in the house full-time to double up in order to keep a room in reserve. A better solution is to allow kids "squatter's rights." They use the room while it's empty, but when the visiting child is in residence, they double up.
- *Does a child who is living in the house have to share a room with a visiting child?* If space is limited, yes.
- *Should a combined family move to new housing so that no one feels as if he or she is moving into someone else's home?* Ideally, yes. Moving into a new home eliminates some territorial issues (although clearly not all). It means that the space is neutral in the sense that it belongs to no one side of the family.
- *Should a visiting child use the household toys that belong to the stepsibling, rather than bring his own along?* It's impractical to expect a nonresidential child to bring all his belongings with him each time he visits. Keep duplicates of the important things in both houses, and negotiate what will be shared.

Deciding these issues is a matter of economics, but fair decisions also require common sense, patience, and respect for all parties. Along with these general rules of thumb, you need to use your own judgment to see if they apply to your family.

Children Who Do Not Live with the Parent Full-Time

In many situations, custody arrangements provide for children to live with the noncustodial parent only on weekends or vacations. Even when children spend part of each week with each parent, the part-time arrangement creates special challenges. Here are some ideas for making these children feel like a full part of the family even when they aren't full-time residents:

Great Idea!

Steal a trick from preschools. If space is tight and you need to create private space for the belongings of visiting stepchildren, have a series of cubbies, each marked with the individual child's name.

- *Every child needs to have some area that is clearly defined as her own.* You may not be able to provide each child with a private room. That may not be possible or preferable—and that's true whether or not you're part of a blended family. But you can find other solutions. If a child does not live in the house regularly, give her a drawer in a bureau or shelf in a closet, and clearly mark that place as hers. It's a spot for her to store her stuff. It should be off-limits to the other children.

- *Symbolism is important.* Keep certain things like the child's toothbrush in the bathroom at all times, whether he's there or not. You want to make clear to him and his stepsiblings that this home is his, too. Change the sheets, give him clean towels, but make him feel at home and not like a guest.

- *Make rules for sharing.* If a child does not live in the house full-time and will be staying in the room of a child who does, it's reasonable to set ground rules for what may be used and what is off-limits. You want both kids to feel that you respect their belongings. It's fair to insist that they share some things—the room telephone, television set, books, and so on. But it's also all right to permit the resident child to mark some of her things as off-limits, just as she would if the child were living full-time in the house. Similarly, the visiting child can reserve some of his belongings as private and keep duplicates of some items in both houses. You need to accommodate the emotional needs of both the resident and nonresident child.

- *Make each child part of the decision-making process.* When all stepsibs are involved in decisions about what rooms and belongings will be shared, they "own" the result. It wasn't imposed on them, and they learn to work together as a team. That's critical in developing a strong family relationship. Within the framework of what is possible, have them work out the details of which side of the room they would prefer and what kind of decorating scheme they want for the room (it

Great Idea!

If stepsibs are going to share a room, both kids need to feel like equal owners of the space. Repaint and redecorate the room so it reflects both of their tastes and neither child feels like a visitor.

doesn't have to be matching). Allow flexibility for negotiation and changes if necessary at some later point. To reduce tensions, take practical steps like providing earphones for listening to music and directional lights next to each bed for reading.

- *Talk, talk, and then talk some more.* Encourage stepsibs to talk about their feelings about room assignments. Resentment and fears are common and to be expected; talk them through. The stepsibs may have suggestions that will work for your family. You can't sweep these feelings under the rug.

Stepsibs Sharing a Room

The rules in force for helping siblings share a room are even more important when stepsibs suddenly become roomies. When that happens, it's more important than ever before that each child have a sense of privacy.

This change will be more difficult if one family moves into the home of the other. Territorial issues immediately arise. It's preferable for the new combined family to move into new quarters so that no one feels displaced or like an intruder. But that's not always possible, so it's important to communicate openly and honestly. Acknowledge the emotions from all the stepsibs—those who are moving in and those who are being asked to share what had previously been their own home.

If possible, within the existing house, create space for each child to have his own room, maybe using the attic or the basement. Of course, even if you can carve out the space, be prepared for comparisons of square footage and cries of "His room is bigger!" The solution? Have the kids agree on a timetable for switching rooms so that each child has an opportunity for the bigger space. Every six months? Every year? Even if they agree on a schedule, you may find that when the time comes for the switch, they prefer to stay where they are. If all agree, accept their decision.

If separate rooms are not possible, you need to work together as a family to determine who should be roommates. If the stepsibs are all the same gender, then you have to decide whether to match the kids by age,

Stepsiblings' relationships may actually improve after the birth of a half-sibling. The new baby is the one relative in the blended family who has a connection to all the kids.

family, or common interests. Remember, none of this is set in stone. But it should be agreed that everyone will give the arrangements a fair chance. Set a date to review how things are going and, if necessary, move people around.

His, Hers, and Theirs

Bringing a new baby into a combined family sparks a new round of sibling issues—but frequently positive ones. Unlike stepsibs, the new baby is someone who belongs to everyone. Some stepparents find they actually are closer to their stepkids after the birth of a new baby in the combined family because they are now more focused on kids in general. The adults may be especially touched by how much love is shared among the kids. And for the baby, as the youngest, he will most likely be nurtured by his older half-sibs, plus his parents.

But be prepared for the usual sibling rivalry that accompanies the birth of any new baby in a family. The step component may exacerbate it, but it's not unreasonable that any kid will be concerned about the new "interloper." They are likely to have several concerns:

- *How will it affect the family dynamic?* Be honest. Things will change, but change can be good. Yes, a new baby demands a lot of time and attention, but a baby can also be a lot of fun. Often a new baby brings a blended family closer together, as the child is the one relative they all share. And the older sibling will enjoy the love and devotion offered by a younger brother or sister.
- *Will the stepparent love this new baby even more than me?* Admittedly, it's probably true that you will find more satisfaction raising your biological child than your stepchild. Still, as the parent, you need to reassure all the older kids in the family that the baby will not supplant them in your heart. Pay attention to the big kids as well as the baby.
- *Will my stepparent still have time for me? How will the baby affect my daily life?* Unquestionably, babies take up a lot of time. Juggling isn't easy, but it's critical for the family that you make some one-on-one time with the older sibs, preferably without the baby.

- *Why does everyone pay so much attention to the baby and not to me?*
  Explain that babies are cute and naturally draw attention, just as she
  did when she was a baby. But make time to focus on the older sib.

Don't rely too heavily on the older half-siblings to be baby-sitters for
the younger kids or new baby. If the older siblings are mature and the
appropriate age, it's reasonable to ask them to baby-sit as part of their
familial responsibilities. But if you expect too much, resentment can
grow.

CHAPTER 12

When to Seek Help

*S*ibling rivalry is inevitable. But don't be overly anxious about it. Sibling rivalry can be healthy. Competition, within reason, can be useful. Brothers and sisters motivate each other.

Yet there are days when sibs can barely say a civil word to each other. In fact, it sometimes feels as if there are weeks, even months, when any interaction between siblings prompts an argument. It can be difficult to decide whether your family's sibling issues are within the range of normal or it might be useful to seek outside help.

One way to begin is to keep a journal for at least two weeks. It will give you a clearer view of what's happening. Review the journal and look for troublesome patterns:

- Is every mealtime disrupted?
- Are all car rides lessons in parental peacekeeping?
- Are there any occasions when the siblings play well together?
- Are the arguments one-sided, or do they leave one child constantly demoralized?
- Do the fights frequently end in physical violence?
- Is one child feeling isolated or embarrassed?
- Is one child afraid of his sibling?

It's not just whether every day produces some sibling spat. That's not unusual. It's the intensity and feel of the arguments:

- *Look for trigger points*—If you know what provokes arguments, you may be able to stop them before they start. Do they occur most fre-

quently around dinnertime when kids are tired and hungry? Around bedtime when parents are at the end of their patience? Are mornings tough because of the rush to get off to work and school? Do arguments erupt during transition times, for example, when moving the children from day care to home?

- *Check the sensibilities of each child to make sure that the disagreements aren't taking a toll*—Is one child constantly being demoralized or being emotionally harassed? You need to look at both angles. Why is she vulnerable? And why is the other child deliberately hurting his sibling? Or is he? Is one child overreacting because of other issues in her life?

- *Note what methods you use to reduce sibling rivalry and how effective they are*—Does one child still feel neglected even after you made sure to give him individual attention? Is a sibling feeling that he can't measure up to the accomplishments of his brother or sister despite more frequent doses of praise from you?

- *Keep track of what else is going on in the family's life*—Are sibling disagreements more likely to erupt on days when the kids have after-school activities? When parents have to work late? Before tests in school? Did they escalate when a parent or grandparent got ill or a crisis erupted at work?

You will need to be a detective to understand the situation and make adjustments. If, however, you can't resolve the problems on your own, the journal will be useful when you seek outside help.

Can You Handle It?

There's no shame in asking for help. We tell our kids that a sign of maturity is to get help when you need it. So if you're concerned about the relationship between your children, you may want to consider seeking assistance. But you may be able to resolve some of the problems on your own. Try these steps:

- *Talk to each child separately*—Pick a quiet time to talk to each youngster about the dynamics in the family. Make it clear that you are not looking to assign blame or listen to a recitation of sibling slights. Instead, you want the child to focus on what prompts the arguments and how she feels about them. Some questions you might ask include, Does your child feel overwhelmed or out-argued each time? Does she feel her sibling takes advantage of her? Appropriates her belongings without asking? Intrudes too much? Doesn't understand her? Takes up too much parental time?

- *Call a family meeting*—Calmly, at a time when no one is rushed or angry, meet together as a family and point out your concerns. Ask for the siblings' input on what is going on between them. This is not to be a blame session but a conversation about what you, the parent, see and what they, the children, see. You may be surprised that they don't think their sibling relationship problems are a big deal. They may not understand your frustrations or concerns. This meeting should not be treated as an opportunity to reveal any confidences exchanged in the individual meetings but instead to get the children to brainstorm and come up with solutions to make the relationship work better and more harmoniously.
- *Post a chart where the kids can see it*—This is not for punishment. It's to show the children concrete evidence that their squabbling has gotten out of hand. Mark down every encounter for a week—and then review the results with the kids. They may not realize how often they argue.
- *Praise good behavior*—Catch the kids playing nicely, and tell them how much you appreciate their behavior.
- *Make adjustments*—Working with your children, adjust daily routines that seem to spark sibling problems. For example, everyone may have to get up earlier to avoid the pressures of the morning rush.

Seeking Outside Help

You should consider seeking outside help in the following situations:

- There has been no improvement after six weeks of trying to reduce tensions and build the self-esteem of each child.
- The fighting is constant and is physically or emotionally damaging.

At Wit's End

"It seems to me that we have to draw the line in sibling rivalry whenever rivalry goes out of bounds into destructive behavior of a physical or verbal kind. The principle needs to be this: whatever the reasons for your feelings, you will have to find civilized solutions."

—Selma H. Fraiberg, child psychoanalyst

Great Idea!

Parenting is a tough job. Consider seeking outside help if you find you are overwhelmed by the demands of caring for your children. When parental stress levels are high, children often react by arguing more with each other.

- The children are exhibiting other behavior problems.
- You feel that you just can't handle it anymore.

Some Sources of Help

There are several places to find help for your family. Sometimes just talking to other parents helps to put the situation in perspective. You may find that your kids' behavior isn't that unusual.

Another way to find support and help is to surf the Internet and visit some parenting websites (see Resources). You may find some helpful information from those who are also in the trenches. Just remember to carefully consider any information you find on the Internet. You don't know how carefully it has been vetted. When reading advice on the Web, trust your instincts and judge how well it applies to your children.

Other sources of help include professionals:

- Your children's pediatrician, who can recommend a therapist if necessary
- Your clergy
- Social service agencies—for a referral, check with your health care provider or call the local medical association
- Your children's classroom teachers or the school psychologist

Raising siblings is challenging, exciting, demanding, satisfying, and ultimately the most rewarding job you'll ever have. At some point, you may need help or an outside perspective. Just as we encourage our children to seek assistance when they need it, don't hesitate or be embarrassed if you feel like you need guidance. It's an act of love.

As you navigate the sometimes treacherous waters of raising more than one, don't let the demands of the job overshadow the joys. You are helping to build relationships among your children that will give them lifelong comfort and support. Enjoy!

Resources

Books

Faber, Adele, and Elaine Mazlish. *Siblings Without Rivalry.* New York: Avon, 1998.

Samalin, Nancy. *Loving Each One Best: A Caring and Practical Approach to Raising Siblings.* New York: Bantam, 1997.

Websites

http://iparentingmedia.com
Pregnancy and parenting information.

http://npin.org
Website of the National Parenting Information Network. Research-based information about the process of parenting and about family involvement in education.

www.babycenter.com
Pregnancy and parenting information.

www.parentcenter.com
Parenting information.

www.parenting.com
Pregnancy and parenting information.

www.parenting.org
Website of the Girls and Boys Town National Resource and Training Center. Information on the day-to-day caretaking, guidance, and development of children.

www.parentingresources.ncjrs.org
Information on school violence, child development, home schooling, organized sports, child abuse, and the juvenile justice system. Sponsored by the Coordinating Council on Juvenile Justice and Delinquency Prevention.

www.parentstages.com
Information about parenting, beginning in pregnancy.

www.tnpc.com
Website of the National Parenting Center. Parenting information from a variety of authorities.

Organizations

International MOMS Club
Nonprofit support group for mothers at home of all ages. There are chapters all across the United States. Visit www.momsclub.org.

Stepfamily Association of America
National nonprofit membership organization dedicated to successful stepfamily living. Write to 650 J Street, Suite 205, Lincoln, NE 68508; call 800-735-0328; or visit www.saafamilies.org.

Index